Preaching Parables to Postmoderns

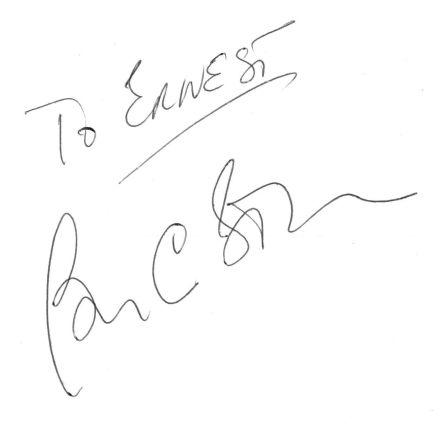

Other Titles in
Fortress Resources for Preaching

~

Preaching Parables
to Postmoderns

Brian C. Stiller

Fortress Press
Minneapolis

Cover art: *Prodigal Son* by Einar Forseth, 1952. Copyright © 2004 Artists Rights Society (ARS, New York / BUS, Stockholm). Used by permission. Photo © Victoria & Albert Museum, London/Art Resource, NY. Used by permission.

Scripture quotations are the author's own translation unless otherwise noted.

Scripture quotations from the New Revised Standard Version of the Bible (NRSV) are copyright © 1989 by the Division of Christian Education of the National Council of the Churches of Christ in the United States of America and are used by permission.

Scripture quotations from the Revised Standard Version of the Bible (RSV) are copyright © 1946, 1952, 1971 by the Division of Christian Education of the National Council of the Churches of Christ in the United States of America and are used by permission.

Scripture from the Holy Bible, New International Version® is copyright © 1973, 1978, 1984 by International Bible Society and is used by permission of Zondervan Publishing House. All rights reserved.

Library of Congress Cataloging-in-Publication Data
Stiller, Brian.
  Preaching parables to postmoderns / Brian C. Stiller.
      p. cm. — (Fortress resources for preaching)
  Includes bibliographical references.
  ISBN 0-8006-3713-5 (alk. paper)
  1. Jesus Christ—Parables—Homiletical use. 2. Postmodernism—Religious aspects—Christianity. I. Title. II. Series.
  BT375.3.S75 2005
  251—dc22
                              2004024820

The paper used in this publication meets the minimum requirements of American National Standard for Information Sciences—Permanence of Paper for Printed Library Materials, ANSI Z329.48-1984.

Manufactured in the U.S.A.

09   08   6   7   8   9   10

Contents

Preface

PREACHERS, IN THEIR CALL TO PREACH THE SCRIPTURES, are not only charged with the responsibility of speaking its truth but of speaking in such a way that people of this age and culture understand. To do this, the preacher builds a bridge between today's people and the gospel of both testaments. For some, this task is more difficult than for others. Preaching to those living in an inner-city housing project is far removed from an outpost mission in the two-thirds world. Each community has its own way of thinking and attaches different values to symbols of its own making.

For those called to preach to a generation raised on MTV and late-night comedians or those rooted in various economic cultures—from government-sponsored jobs overseen by union bosses to entrepreneurial dot-com companies—or generations stretching from high school students to "freedom fifty-fivers," the task is enormous. When one adds to that the complexity of a radical shift in underlying intellectual and cultural assumptions, the task of preaching becomes even more complicated.

Although we believe that the Word by its nature is powerful in reshaping lives, we still wonder how we can meet the multiple needs of a highly pluralistic and diverse people, some of whom have been raised on Bible stories and others who cannot tell a biblical saying from an honored maxim. No longer is biblical literacy to be assumed. No longer can it be taken for granted that those who attend worship accept basic theological affirmations. It is to this mixed crowd that a preacher comes weekly.

Therefore, one of the most significant questions that preachers ask in this changing and radically secular age is, *How are people to understand the Bible if they have less and less knowledge of it or its stories?*

It is not only critical for preaching ministers to search for strategic ways to appeal to contemporary generations, it is also important to find ways of speaking the biblical message so those who are biblically illiterate can understand. As well, if people do not read or understand the Bible, the task of the preacher is made even more demanding—for the loss of biblical knowledge leads to an unfamiliarity not only with biblical names and events but also with its underlying ideals and moral impulses.

Along with this loss of biblical understanding, the assumptions of modernity are challenged by a postmodern paradigm that reworks René Descartes' starting point of reason as being the foundation for discovering truth to include intuition and experience as lenses through which truth can also be discovered.

One result of this reworking of the starting point of knowing has been a blooming of interest in ideas loosely called "spirituality." While this may at times lead to all sorts of excesses, it has inadvertently opened doors to Christian faith, providing opportunities for new initiatives in Christian outreach and evangelization.

The common form of public discourse that cuts across all lines of ethnicity, culture, economic or social status, age, or gender is the story, be it modern or postmodern. Stories grip the mind and heart and not only provide a vision of God but are themselves the stuff of the Spirit, by which the work of our redeeming God is done. In short, we can speak to a people, sometimes suspicious, sometimes bored, and often intellectually lazy, with an approach and content that sneaks past usual forms of resistance.

In short, it is important that preachers understand this shift in cultural thinking and become adept at using Jesus' parables as windows through which the interested and even the disinterested can peer. This book is designed to speak to such issues.

1

Postmodernity

"I don't think we're in Kansas anymore," commented Dorothy to Toto in *The Wizard of Oz*. Living in the early years of the twenty-first century, we might experience a similar sense of dislocation. As Dorothy realized something had changed, so critical writers of the past quarter-century remind us that the assumptions of much of the twentieth century—what is called "modernity"[1]—are not as they once were. The shift—called "postmodernity"—is away from previous philosophical underpinnings to something quite different, ideas that fundamentally alter how we think about what is true. Although there is a growing debate over what these words mean and their respective values, there is a widely held consensus that the theories of the modern era are no longer taken as the only basis on which truth is to be learned or life is to be lived.

Here I want to point out the shift from modernity to postmodernity and to examine the meaning of postmodernity for purposes of preaching.

The Nature of Change

The term *postmodern* is a framework for thinking about our contemporary world.[2] It also is a simple way of saying that the world has changed. For our purposes in preaching, the question we want to have answered is this: What has changed and to what degree has that change affected the way people may think and respond to the Scriptures and thus preaching?

That we live in a world referred to as *postmodern* is not to say that what we have known as *modern* no longer exists. Historical

1

movements do not move from one totally encompassing idea to another. Rather, they flow from one into the other. There is never a total end to one and a clear-cut beginning to another. We do not wake up one day with life having so changed that what has been no longer is. Life changes over time, and as it does, society gradually comes to think differently about its world. What emerges stands on the shoulders of what went before—or, to put it another way, the plant of this age grows out of the soil and ingredients of the past, which in turn become the hubris of the next stage of growth.

What concerns us here is the nature of that change and the resulting changes in values and priorities. In preaching, if a congregation is rural, made up of those whose daily work is in agriculture or who at least are surrounded by metaphors of that world, we will search for different ways of speaking than if the church is made up of stockbrokers and middle- to high-end corporate managers. Because these groups see life through different cultural glasses and use different figures of speech, the sermon must use what helps congregants connect to the scriptural passage.

Given this, the question is, In what way does this generation—be they farmers or stockbrokers—differ in language from the former generation? Answering this question is an important task of the preacher.

The Premodern and Modern Ages

From first-century Palestine through to the seventeenth century, revelation was the primary means by which life was to be interpreted. During this *premodern* age the church—at least in the Western world—dominated. The early church—reshaped by the Roman emperor Constantine, who made Christianity the culturally accepted faith—became the ultimate authority in the Holy Roman Empire. Exploration, intellectual inquiry, and political rule found authority within the church. That changed during the Renaissance, "the grandmother of modernity and mother of the Enlightenment" (Grenz 1996, 60). René Descartes (1596–1650) looked for a philosophical starting point other than God, an assertion that inevitably raised the question, "Where did God come from?" Descartes' formula for determining the starting point for philosophical reflection was, *Cogito, ergo sum*: "I think, therefore I am." This simple but profound assertion brought into play a new way of seeing life that profoundly influenced Western thinking, by building its starting point of inquiry on rationality rather than revelation.

The wave of change continued as Martin Luther challenged the absolute and encompassing power of the church by asserting that we come to Christ by faith, not by the mediating influence of the church and her appointees. This wall of the premodern age began to crack as religion started to lose its dominant role in the life of the people.

Reason, an idea Descartes borrowed from Augustine, became the cornerstone of the modern era. Reason established the rules and criteria for understanding reality. Ideas were tested through the grid of rationality. Only by reason, it was argued, could humans understand themselves and their surrounding cosmos and in turn re-create the world for purposes of human betterment.[3] The way of doing this varied from philosopher to philosopher.[4] While reason was the operating formula, *faith in self* was its underlying assumption. "I exist, therefore . . ." puts not only the emphasis but the focus of trust on "self." This "I" can be in isolation as the autonomous self or it can be in community, but in the end there is nothing beyond to which one can appeal for help. In effect, God was replaced as the primary source of truth. With God set aside and self now at the center, it was natural to assert the potential of self. Anything previously regarded as true was to be examined through the new microscope of reason. Not only was the self regarded as having potential, but it was exalted in its moral capabilities. With God less and less in the picture for both the human self and the surrounding cosmos, the world was seen more as a machine, with the tragic result that humanity became but a cog in the machine of a God-absent world.[5]

The principled framework of the modern age was reason. Within that framework developed a confidence that humans could change the world by understanding it. This rested on the assumption that *nature* was itself orderly, to be discerned by laws that were not only intelligible but, by way of human reason and ingenuity, could be controlled and subdued.

In effect, human reason had "dethroned the reverence for external authority as an arbiter of truth that had characterized the medieval and Reformation period" (Grenz 1996, 68). Appealing to the Bible or church authorities no longer sufficed. The human self could make claims without the need to refer to something outside of human reason. Nature was understood as *autonomous*.

Progress was seen as inevitable: Life was moving forward and upward. The end result would be freedom, happiness, and the well-being of people living within an orderly society. Given the barbarous nature of the Middle Ages and the modernist view that the previous age had been controlled by religious superstition, which resulted in its many wars and brutal practices, optimism flourished in this newfound Age of Reason.

Modernity had its most serious impact upon religion; indeed, it challenged the very basis of Christian faith, which had as it starting point the external God. Nature was seen as antithetical to revelation. What one believed by "revelation" was not to be taken seriously. Belief was regarded as "personal." It was seen as not being scientifically true and, therefore, illegitimate in having a place in public, being confined to the privacy of one's community or mind. In that way religion and faith were "privatized" by modern thought.

Not surprisingly, belief in the Bible was undermined and by none more devastatingly than Charles Darwin and his view of evolutionary naturalism in which science was seen to be the explanation for all of life, including human origin.[6] The Bible, by contrast, because of its claims about the origin of life which could not pass the scrutiny of empirical observation, was judged to be myth and superstition at best, and blatantly false at worst.

Modernity's vision was based on a trust that knowledge would liberate people from tyranny even as science was to overcome nature, freeing civilizations from want, wars, and the unpredictability of the surrounding world. Organization would oversee societies and economies, liberating society from "the irrationalities of myth, religious superstition, release from the arbitrary use of power as well as from the dark side of our own human natures" (Harvey, 12). The modern era "was, above all, a secular movement that sought the demystification and desacralization of knowledge and social organization in order to liberate human beings from their chains" (13).

In the early years of the twentieth century the modernist and optimistic mood of inevitability and invincibility was punctured.[7] Death camps, death squads, and death bombs—tools of modernity—showed how vulnerable was this underbelly of optimism.

Lurking behind the well-honed assumptions of modernity was the age-old human impulse to oppress and dominate. Nothing much had changed. The regimes of Joseph Stalin, Adolf Hitler, or Pol Pot made that clear. The awe-inspiring notions of fraternity, liberty, and equality that characterized the late nineteenth and early twentieth centuries were found wanting where it really mattered. The lust to dominate and control had not been dissolved by the rhetoric of universal brotherhood.

The Postmodern Experiment

Postmodernism, the child of modernity, incubated during the first half of the twentieth century and was born in the latter part of the twentieth century. Some postmodern ideas grew of modern notions while others—in almost an angry sort of way—were a backlash against modernity's triumphal assertions. Douglas Coupland, who first used the term "Generation X" to describe a late-twentieth-century generation, expresses his inner struggle in the last page of *Life after God.*

> Now—here is my secret: I speak to you with an openness of heart that I doubt I shall ever achieve again, so I pray that you are in a quiet room as you hear these words. My secret is that I need God—that I am sick and can no longer make it alone. I need God to help me give, because I no longer seem to be capable of giving; to help me be kind, as I no longer seem capable of kindness; to help me love, as I seem beyond being able to love. (Coupland, 360)

It can also be heard in philosophy from the angry words of Friedrich Nietzsche. The twentieth-century German philosopher, in *Thus Spake Zarathustra*, in which the mythical figure Zarathustra preached the death of God and the emergence of the superman, "spelled the beginning of the end of modernity and the inauguration of the gestation period of postmodernity" (Grenz 1996, 83). In *On Truth and Lie in an Extra-Moral Sense*, Nietzsche wrote:

> What then is truth? A mobile army of metaphors, metonyms, and anthropomorphism—in short a sum of human relations, which have been enhanced, transposed, and embellished poetically and

rhetorically, and which after long use seem firm, canonical, and obligatory to a people; truths are illusions of which one has forgotten that this is what they are; metaphors which are worn out and without sensuous power; coins which have lost their pictures and now matter only as metal, no longer as coins. (Nietzsche, 46–47)

Educators and leaders of today were influenced by the antiestablishment movement that flourished in the late 1960s. Antagonistic to the scientific and bureaucratic structures of centralized power, countercultural movements reacted to the dominance of bureaucracies and governments. Students, aided by drugs and financed by the wealth of parents, spilled into the streets of many cities in Europe and North America angrily demanding a deconstruction of the establishment. Technology, a symbol of the modern-scientific mind, became the means that enabled folk heroes of the 1960s and 1970s—philosophers speaking often by way of music—to spread their anti-Western/anti-Enlightenment rhetoric. Disparaging capitalistic and political imperialism symbolized by a dishonest president (Nixon) and a foreign war going bad (Vietnam), the power of this antimodern force helped bring about a world reshaping that today we call postmodernity.

How did this turn so quickly? What brought it about? As God had been questioned as the source of truth in the late years of the premodern era, in the late years of the modern era reason got its turn. *Rationality* as the cornerstone of the modern era was challenged as, centuries before, *revelation* had been challenged.

Characteristics of Postmodernity

The essential ingredients of postmodernity point out the underlying shift taking place today. These include the following.

1. Reason, the fundamental building block of modern thought, is rejected as the only prime means to discover truth. Philosophical thought has opened the door to increasingly considering experience and intuition as being avenues to truth. This has led to seeing truth as not that which is true *out there*, but that which is *interior*, so that self both defines and articulates what the self believes is true.

2. Postmodernity also rejects the modern assertion that truth is objective.[8] For a postmodernist, truth is the construct of the one making the declaration. Meaning is but a human phenomenon. The conversation of three umpires outlines three ways of viewing truth. One says, "There are balls and strikes, and I call them as they are." The other responds, "No, balls and strikes are as I see them." The postmodern disagrees. "They ain't nothing 'til I call them."[9] The working phrase is "personal perspective" and not "true truth," a frequent phrase of Francis Schaeffer, a Christian apologist of the 1970s. Because experience and opinion shape what we hold to be true, "truth" has been compromised by the very nature of one making the assertion. It may be true for the person, the argument goes, but who is to say it is true for another?[10]

3. Postmoderns dismiss authorities who, by their positions of power, use "truth" to oppress and advance their personal agendas. History, because it is written by the conquerors, is denied as being an accurate description of what took place. As history is rejected, "political correctness" becomes the mantra. Since no one can presume that their narrative is anything other than their own, there is no narrative that can presume to speak for anyone but the one making the assertion. The growing paranoia over keeping within one's own verbal or presumptive space becomes a preoccupation.

4. As objective truth is rejected so is the metanarrative—a grand and sweeping story that gives meaning to life and serves to answer the larger questions of human existence. Thus the Bible—with its wide landscape of the history of God and creation, a story explaining the human saga—is dismissed. Again, the assumption is that the narrative was written to serve those in power.

5. As truth is relative, all ideas are considered to be of equal value. Allan Bloom notes a deep conviction that "relativism is necessary to openness; and this is the virtue, the only virtue, which all primary education for more than fifty years has dedicated itself to inculcating. Openness—and the relativism that makes it the only plausible stance in the face of various claims to truth . . . is the great insight of our times" (Bloom, 26).

6. In populist terms, postmodernity is driven by a concern for the therapeutic. If personal well-being is all important, then finding ways to shape one's self into well-being is the preoccupying concern. As Roger Lundin comments, "A therapeutic culture is one

in which questions of ultimate concern—about the nature of the good, the meaning of truth and the existence of God—are taken to be unanswerable and hence, in some fundamental sense, insignificant" ("The Pragmatics of Postmodernity," in Phillips and Okholm, 31). Alasdair MacIntyre agrees: "Truth has been displaced as a value and replaced by psychological effectiveness" (MacIntyre, 31).

This brief outline of postmodern thought provides a basis on which to consider the role of the parables in preaching. But first let us examine the nature of the literary parabolic form.

2

Parables:
A Window on Truth for Postmoderns

PEOPLE LOVE A STORY. Watch children and adults come to attention when a minister makes a shift in the sermon with, "Let me tell you a story." It is not surprising that the best-known parts of the Old Testament tend to be stories: Noah and the ark, Jonah and the "whale," David and Goliath. The same is true for the New Testament, beginning with Jesus' birth in a manger. Apart from these stories of history, what people tend to remember from the Bible are the grand stories, the parables of Jesus such as the Good Samaritan or the Prodigal Son. Mark, in speaking about Jesus' teaching, said, ". . . he did not speak to them except in parables" (4:34). Indeed, a full third of Jesus' teachings in the Synoptic Gospels were parables, with more than sixty-seven examples of similes and metaphors in the Gospels.

Definition of *Parable*

The English word *parable* comes from the Greek *parabole*, which in turn comes from "other" and "speaking," combining to mean "speaking otherwise than one seems to speak" (Hultgren, 12). The Hebrew derivation is *mashal*, literally translated "to set aside" or "to throw beside."

The New Testament parables of Jesus are unique, without parallel. First, a parable compares two unlike things and, as a literary device, acts in three ways: comparative, similar, or parallel. Second, whether short or long, its intent is both to *inform*, by describing some form of reality, and *affect*, by providing a picture. Third, its genius is in its ability to disarm the listener and persuade, catching one by surprise. Its vivid story or compelling intrigue makes it hard to ignore. Fourth, in part its impact is because it "comes suddenly, usually before people are able to defend themselves against its message" (Robert Stein, "The Genre of the Parables," in Longenecker, 47–48).

Parables told in the first-century Jewish culture of Palestine came from and were rooted in oral tradition. Many listeners could not read, so the way they learned was to memorize. Parables thus fit into the patterns of that age. A parable, like a joke, is short; if it is too long, it cannot be remembered. Thus, in a literary device when memory was critical to learning, brevity was essential.

Parables were also concrete, not abstract. In the Hebrew tradition, the more concrete the story, the more it assisted the hearer in locking it into memory. The words and illustrations of Jesus were familiar to the culture: He spoke of everyday people who would be recognized in the marketplaces and rural areas of Palestine. Jesus did not speak of psychological factors that give us insight as to why people did what they did. In the story of the vineyard keeper who hired people throughout the day and paid them all the same wage, Jesus did not tell us why the keeper chose do that, he just did.

In the study of parables, scholars divide parables into various categories. Arland J. Hultgren notes two basic types of parables: the narrative parables, which include narration and convey the "once upon a time" feel; and the similitude parables, which, though they do contain narration, use an "is like" reference. It is within these two forms that he identifies thirty-eight biblical units that he views as being parables (Hultgren, 3, 6).

Grant R. Osborne expands Hultgren's listing of New Testament parables to include:
1. proverbs—"Physician, heal yourself" (Luke 4:23);
2. metaphors—"You are the light of the world" (Matt. 5:14);
3. similes—"I send you out like sheep in the midst of wolves" (Matt. 10:16);
4. figurative sayings—new wine in old wineskins (Luke 5:36-38);
5. story parables, which are fictional narratives—the Ten Virgins (Matt. 25:1-13), the Persistent Widow (Luke 18:1-8), the Barren Fig Tree (Luke 13:6-9);
6. illustrative or example stories in which the parable models what is appropriate conduct, as in the Good Samaritan (Luke 10:29-37);

7. allegorical parables with several points—the Parable of the
    Sower (Mark 4:1-9; 13-20). (Osborne, 236)

Relationship of Jesus' Parables to the Hebrew Tradition

Biblical scholars vary on whether or not Jesus' parables are unique
or if they are like stories told in the region during the Old Testament
and intertestamental period.[1]

In the Old Testament *mashalim* is used to define various literary
forms—as a maxim: "like mother, like daughter" (Ezek. 16:44); a
byword: "You have made us a byword among the nations, a laugh-
ingstock among the peoples" (Ps. 44:14); a riddle: "I will open my
mouth in a parable; I will utter dark sayings from of old" (Ps. 78:2);
a parable: Nathan's story of the poor man's lamb (2 Sam. 12:1-4);
and an allegory: "Son of man, set forth an allegory and tell the house
of Israel a parable" (Ezek. 17:2-10 NIV) (Robert Stein, "The Genre of
the Parables," in Longenecker, 39–47).

New Testament scholar Craig Evans locates ten *mashalim* in the
Old Testament that loosely resemble those of Jesus.[2] He also notes
that the most famous of Old Testament *mashalim* is the Parable of
the Ewe Lamb, which Nathan the prophet uses to confront King
David about his sin:

> There were two men in a certain town, one rich and the other poor.[2]
> The rich man had a very large number of sheep and cattle, [3]but the
> poor man had nothing except one little ewe lamb he had bought.
> He raised it, and it grew up with him and his children. It shared
> his food, drank from his cup and even slept in his arms. It was like
> a daughter to him. [4]Now a traveler came to the rich man, but the
> rich man refrained from taking one of his own sheep or cattle to
> prepare a meal for the traveler who had come to him. Instead, he
> took the ewe lamb that belonged to the poor man and prepared it
> for the one who had come to him. (2 Sam. 12:1b-4 NIV)

David is outraged that anyone would do such a cursed thing and
exclaims, "The man who has done this deserves to die!" (v. 5). It is
then he learns that he, David, is the man.

Evans lists[3] other Old Testament *mashalim*: the Parable of the
Two Brothers (2 Sam. 14:4-7); the Parable of the Escaped Prisoner
(1 Kings 20:38-43); the Fable of the Thistle and the Cedar (2 Kings

14:8-10); the Song of the Vineyard (Isa. 5:1-7); the Riddle or Parable of the Eagles and Vine (Ezek. 17:2-10); a funeral lament (Ezek. 19:1-9); the Parable of the Vine (Ezek. 19:10-14); the Parable of the Forest Fire (Ezek. 20:45-49 [Heb. 21:1-5]); the Parable of the Seething Pot (Ezek. 24:2-5).

As well as the existence of Old Testament *mashal*, during the postbiblical period (following the Old Testament books) there were a few parables, most of which come to us from the Dead Sea Scrolls of Qumran, and parables that would have been in circulation during the time of Jesus. These parables, judgmental by nature, told stories as if they were facts so as to deceive the hearer by making it appear that an actual event was being recounted. Those in Ezekiel contained allegorical elements and were addressed to the monarchs or leaders. The dreams were not for teaching purposes but seen as messages from God, albeit needing deciphering.

For Evans, Jewish parables of the postbiblical period "are right at home in first-century Jewish Palestine. In most respects Jesus' parables are not unique. Their emphasis on the kingdom of God roughly parallels the rabbis' emphasis on God as king, though with important differences. Jesus' parables begin with introductory phrases such as 'to what may this be compared?' or 'the kingdom of God is like'" (Evans, "Parables in Early Judaism," in Longenecker, 72–73).

New Testament scholar Craig L. Blomberg notes three reasons why Jesus' parables differ from the rabbinic tradition. (1) The rabbinic tradition generally reinforces the conventional wisdom or biblical exegesis, which is in contrast to the "subversive" strategy of Jesus' parables. "For the most part, Jesus' parables subvert Jewish tradition, whereas rabbinic stories reinforce it" (Blomberg, 67). (2) Many of Jesus' parables make reference to God's kingdom as being inaugurated through his presence. Thus, the distinctiveness of Jesus' parables is neither in their form nor content but in function. (3) Much of the rabbinic texts are caught up in interpretation and application, whereas in Jesus' parables there is little of that (Blomberg, 65–68).

James Breech—who carried out an eight-year study of stories extant from the time of Alexander the Great (ca. 300 B.C.E.) to Constantine (ca. 300 C.E.)—concludes that "Jesus' parables are dissimilar from all extant contemporary stories" (Breech 1989, 24–25). He notes there are few extant parables by Jesus' Hebrew contemporaries—Hillel (ca. 60 B.C.E.–20 C.E.) and Shammai (ca. 50 B.C.E.–30 C.E.)—to which German scholar Joachim Jeremias agrees: "Jesus' parables are something entirely new. In all the rabbinic literature, not one single parable has come down to us from the period before Jesus; only two similes from Rabbi Hillel who jokingly compared the body with a statue, and the soul with a guest" (Jeremias 1972, 12).

Thus, while the Jewish world was familiar with parables as a means of teaching/exhorting, it seems that little before or after the life and ministry of Jesus—apart from Nathan's parable to King David (2 Sam. 12:1b-4)—matches his parables. The contrast of Jesus' parables and the rabbinic tradition is obvious. Rabbis used the *mashal* in an exegetical form, clarifying and interpreting what they saw the text was saying to the people of Israel. Jesus' parables are complete in and of themselves with little exegesis or clarification required. Though Jesus affirms another's quote of an Old Testament text—as in the Good Samaritan parable (Luke 10:25-37) when the lawyer cites the Old Testament (Deut. 6:5; Lev. 19:18)—his story form had its own life and operated within its own authority.

Biblical scholar Brad Young's conclusion sums it up:

> The parables of Jesus, like their counterparts in the rabbinic literature, are unique. Some teaching forms, such as fables or allegories, are somewhat similar to Gospel and rabbinic parables, but the classic form of story parables, such as those in the Gospels and rabbinic literature, is a distinct type of teaching technique that has no parallel. They do not appear in the Dead Sea Scrolls, the Apocrypha or the Pseudepigrapha. They do appear frequently in talmudic texts. In rabbinic literature, they are always told in Hebrew and not Aramaic. (Young, 271)

Those listening to Jesus were struck by the power in his stories for he taught them "as one having authority, and not as the scribes" (Mark 1:22). The messenger, unique as God-in-humanity, employs a storytelling technique familiar to his people but with a remarkable twist. Jesus goes beyond merely reinforcing biblical maxims and instead introduces revolutionary ideas about God. So, regardless how much the hearer knows about Hebrew writing or theology, he gave little opportunity for people to leave without a response.

The Purpose of the Parable

One is struck by Mark's definition of parabolic purpose, which seems at first to be counterproductive:

> [10]When he was alone, the Twelve and the others around him asked him about the parables. [11]He told them, "The secret of the kingdom of God has been given to you. But to those on the outside everything is said in parables [12]so that,
> > "'they may be ever seeing but never perceiving,
> > and ever hearing but never understanding;
> > otherwise they might turn and be forgiven!'" (4:10-12 NIV)

Matthew's recounting of Jesus' explanation does not seem to be any more helpful.

> [10]The disciples came to him and asked, "Why do you speak to the people in parables?"
> [11]He replied, "The knowledge of the secrets of the kingdom of heaven has been given to you, but not to them. [12]Whoever has will be given more, and he will have an abundance. Whoever does not have, even what he has will be taken from him. [13]This is why I speak to them in parables:
> > "Though seeing, they do not see;
> > though hearing, they do not hear or understand.
> [14]In them is fulfilled the prophecy of Isaiah:
> > "'You will be ever hearing but never understanding;
> > you will be ever seeing but never perceiving.
> [15] For this people's heart has become calloused;
> > they hardly hear with their ears,
> > and they have closed their eyes.
> Otherwise they might see with their eyes,
> > hear with their ears,
> > understand with their hearts
> and turn, and I would heal them.'
> [16]But blessed are your eyes because they see, and your ears because they hear. [17]For I tell you the truth, many prophets and righteous men longed to see what you see but did not see it, and to hear what you hear but did not hear it. . . ." (13:10-17)

Luke follows much along the lines of Mark's analysis.

When he said this, he called out, "He who has ears to hear, let him hear."

⁹His disciples asked him what this parable meant. ¹⁰He said, "The knowledge of the secrets of the kingdom of God has been given to you, but to others I speak in parables, so that,

"'though seeing, they may not see;
though hearing, they may not understand.'" (8:8b-10)

What are we to make of Jesus' seeming attempt to use the parabolic form to increase darkness rather than to illuminate? Why were their hearts hardened and how does a parable harden one to hear the gospel?

Jesus, by way of his preaching, was inviting people to join him in the launch of his kingdom. In the first-century Palestinian world, there were high expectations that the king of the Jews would rule with power, throwing out the Romans and anyone who dared to inflict their rule on Israel. Jesus neither fulfilled those dreams nor were his messages intended to fire those dreams.

In his parables, Jesus allowed no one to remain neutral: People were forced to respond to his call to join him in this new kingdom. Parables were Jesus' way of breaking into resistant minds with insights that stunned his hearers, not only with a surprise and twist but also with shocking wisdom. Regardless of their content, those who didn't hear what they expected refused to hear what he was saying. To understand the parables one has to work at it, and if you don't, you end up not understanding. Pedagogically, in the process of learning, one moves from one level of understanding to a greater level of difficulty, only as one grasps the more elementary levels. Those listening to Jesus—then and today—will move to the more difficult insights of his kingdom only as they learn what is primary.

For those who reject God's life in Jesus—as did the religious leaders—the parable ends up as a judge, and as they continue to reject his insights and claims, the more they are unable to understand him. In that sense, their hearts are further hardened.

Characteristics of the Parables of Jesus

The parables of Jesus are marked by characteristics that set them off as being uniquely the genre of Jesus' preaching. These unique characteristics include the following.

Jesus' parables are earthy.

One is immediately struck with the common and ordinary story world of Jesus. He draws copiously from the immediate world of those who listen: coins, sheep, vineyards, birds, mustard seed, wicked tenants, weddings, and hospitality. Jesus uniquely puts these common images into the parabolic basket, from which he plucks surprising lessons of ethics and kingdom truths. It is important to look for those hidden truths that rise out of the seemingly unimportant details. For example, the father in the Prodigal Son who ran to greet the younger son did so at great loss to his dignity. His running necessitated the lifting of his robes, which meant his bare legs would show, which, for a first-century Hebrew male, was humiliating and socially taboo (Bailey, *Poet and Peasant*, 181).

Parables do not require previous learning.

Parables do not require that the hearer have an arsenal of information to understand either the characters or the plot. The everyday characters and experiences are what the most ordinary of Palestinian residents acquainted with Jewish culture would understand.

The parables of Jesus are direct and concise.

In some stories, Jesus puts his hearers on the spot with a direct and penetrating question (Luke 11:5-7; 14:28; 15:4; 17:7; Matt. 12:11). In contrast to Jewish parables, which serve to elaborate a point in the law, Jesus, by asking for a response, drives home the point in calling for a response:

> [16]And he told them this parable: "The ground of a certain rich man produced a good crop. [17]He thought to himself, 'What shall I do? I have no place to store my crops.'
>
> [18] "Then he said, 'This is what I'll do. I will tear down my barns and build bigger ones, and there I will store all my grain and my goods. [19]And I'll say to myself, "You have plenty of good things laid up for many years. Take life easy; eat, drink and be merry."'
>
> [20]"But God said to him, 'You fool! This very night your life will be demanded from you. Then who will get what you have prepared for yourself?'
>
> [21]"This is how it will be with anyone who stores up things for himself but is not rich toward God." (Luke 12:16-21)

Parables have a unique structure with a major and some minor points.

Most parables will tend to have one main story, while some will have more than one subplot—or mini-story—as in the Prodigal Son: The son who left is forgiven by the father and the self-centered son who stayed is offered that same love. Both stories find their anchor in the larger story of the father's love, but each has its own story line.

Many parables use repetition.

To stress the importance of a major point, a phrase may be used more than once, as in the Parable of the Faithful Servant: "Well done, good and faithful servant! You have been faithful with a few things; I will put you in charge of many things" (Matt. 25:21, 23 NIV).

There is often a conclusion.

Jesus often used a brief phrase such as, "So is he who lays up treasure for himself" (Luke 12:21). Or it may be a question, as he asked the lawyer in the Parable of the Good Samaritan (Luke 10:36): "Who of these three . . . was a neighbor?" It is not so much that the concluding phrase is an interpretation of the parable as it is an application to the wider community. The parable not only informs, it affects. "Interpreters in the past have often so concentrated on the informative dimension that they lost sight of the powerful, affective nature of this literary form" (Robert Stein, "The Genre of the Parables," in Longenecker, 37).

Parables use a surprise element of a reversal of expectation.

Jesus shattered expectations by reversing the norms of the hearer, his ending clashing with where the audience expected the story to go. The difficulty in preaching these stories to today's audience is that they do not understand the meaning of particular words, nor are they able to see how they matter to the understanding of the story. For example, in the prayers of the Pharisee and tax collector, people of Jesus' day assumed he was applauding the careful and complete prayer of the Pharisee. The shock that Jesus was speaking of the tax collector is hard for us to appreciate today, and unless we do, we miss Jesus' point.

Parables often speak to ethical concerns.

Throughout the parables Jesus pushes us to see that his kingdom requires his followers to act differently. His kingdom message is a call to a radically different way of living, be it forgiveness, as in the case of two debtors (Matt. 18:21-35), or reconciliation, as with the prodigal son (Luke 15:11-32).

Parables tend to combine two elements of Jewish tradition.

Jesus brings together two elements, wisdom and eschatology, which are often treated as two separate strains in Jewish culture. In the wisdom tradition, wisdom is seen as being timeless, without respect to any particular period; conversely, the eschatological tradition makes claims regarding the importance of time, not linked to concerns of wisdom. In the Parable of the Ten Maidens (Matt. 25:1-13) Jesus draws the two together: While the wise are prepared, they are prepared for the moment the bridegroom returns. Wisdom is very much linked to the need for an actual arrival or moment. The urgency of wisdom prevailing for the eschatological moment is reinforced by the five who, by not being prepared, are foolish. Jesus ties in the critical matter of being ready—that is, wise—for the time of God's action: "Keep awake, therefore, for you know neither the day nor the hour" (v. 13).

Parables always speak to our vision of God and his means of salvation.

God and salvation are always there, be they in front or lurking in the shadows. In many of Jesus' parables, God is seen as the father with the free gift of salvation. This offer of salvation, by its very presence, in turn requires a response to the God of history. Jesus does not give us a theoretical description of God. Instead, we learn about him through the colorful use of metaphor: a father, a king, a shepherd, owner of a vineyard, or a woman searching for a treasure.

Interpreting the Parables for Preaching

How does a preacher go about studying the parables so as to apply them to the lives of hearers today? To avoid misreading what the parables say, guidelines keep us from the ditch of misinterpretation.

They hold us in the story, faithful to its context, all the while searching out what the listeners of his day would have heard. This is done so that Jesus' first-century words can be translated for the listeners of this age. Critical in handling the text and making it readable for the congregation are nine hermeneutical issues that shape how we move from exegesis to the sermon.

1. Note where the parable is placed within the wider text.

The flow of the text and location of the parable within the wider text tell us what was going on before and after the telling of the story. They also inform us as to whom Jesus is speaking. For example, after an objection by Simon the Pharisee concerning Jesus' allowing a prostitute to wash his feet and anoint him with perfume, Jesus tells the story of two debtors (Luke 7:41-42). That this story is positioned amid a larger story context—the accounts of the remarkable faith of the centurion of Capernaum, the raising of the widow's son, and John the Baptist's question as to whether Jesus was the one they were looking for—is vital to an understanding of its meaning. Also, that he was speaking to a Pharisee provides us with an even deeper understanding of his story.

2. Compare parables to their counterparts in other Synoptic Gospels, noting where each evangelist locates it.

Where more than one evangelist includes a parable in his text, it is valuable to compare both the context of each and how the parable is treated by the evangelist. For example, Luke (19:12-27) and Matthew (25:14-30) each locate the Parable of the Pounds or Talents in different sequences so as to create a different emphasis.

3. Study the structure of the parable.

As a literary device, the parable is constructed to maximize impact with a minimum of words. Ken Bailey, in *Poet and Peasant*, demonstrates how the structure itself points the reader to the key idea or phrase within the parable. He points out four types of literary structures that serve to guide the reader in understanding the story itself:

1. a section of prose that uses the inversion principle for an outline in which the ideas expressed follow an ABCDEF FEDCBA pattern (Dan. 3:13-30);

2. poetical sections in which the ideas are parallel (Bailey points out seven possible patterns) as in AA BB CC;
3. sections of a passage that have a parallel structure in the middle but are encased on either side by prose (Acts 5:1-6);
4. parables in Luke that follow what he calls a *parabolic ballad*, distinct from the others, in which either stepped parallelism or inverted parallelism is used (e.g., Luke 10:30-37). (Bailey, *Poet and Peasant*, 44–75)

4. Identify cultural realities.

The cultural realities are particularly important in unearthing the meaning of a parable. In the Parable of the Unjust Steward (Luke 16:1-13), the understanding of the laws of usury and commission are key to understanding Jesus' message.

5. Discern Jesus' main point.

Even though a parable may have many subpoints, it is important to isolate its main point. It may be located in the introduction or in conversations prior to the actual story or in the epilogue. In parables with more than one significant point, finding the central point is more difficult. In the Parable of the Sower (Matt. 13:1-23; Mark 4:1-20; Luke 8:4-15), though some disagree over whether the main point is found in the sower or in the harvest, both miss the larger context: Jesus is speaking to Jewish religious leaders who reject Jesus and his kingdom.

6. Position parables within the wider array of Jesus' teachings.

While parables are distinct units or stories in and of themselves, they are written and compiled within the wider history of Jesus' life and the text as written by the evangelists. In that sense, they are not stand-alone stories but fit within the larger scheme of the coming of Jesus and his teachings. Once a parable's place is understood within the overall aim of the evangelist, the preacher must make it clear how it relates to the wider message of Jesus. For example, Luke includes the parables on going to war and building a tower within Jesus' radical demands for discipleship. As you count the cost of building a tower or going to war, so he suggests it is important for those who want to follow him also to count the cost.

7. Avoid prooftexting.

Preachers are vulnerable to the temptation of building a doctrine on specific points within a parable without checking on how they relate to the wider text. In the Parable of the Rich Man and Lazarus (Luke 16: 19-31), for example, Jesus speaks about the two being in separate parts of Hades. As interesting as this is, nowhere else in the Gospels is it mentioned that Hades is so divided. To build a theology of the afterlife by way of this "local color" not only distorts the message of the parable, but it ends up framing the afterlife in a way that is not supported anywhere else in the biblical texts.

8. Walk back in time and hear what those in first-century Palestine heard.

In preaching from the parables, it serves the purpose of the sermon if the preacher walks the hearer back in time to the setting of Jesus' telling. Allow the parable to echo within the minds of the listeners, giving them opportunity to appreciate the rich texture of the story. Avoid breaking off a segment of the parable and making it the focus of the message. The entire story needs telling so that the big idea will emerge as the fulcrum around which the story revolves.

Parables are stories of surprise. The stories do not reinforce religious bias; instead, they do the opposite. The preacher needs to put herself or himself into the first-century setting and feel the shock as the story turns a corner, upsetting the expectations of the listener. In the Parable of the Workers (Matt. 20:1-16), when the "eleventh hour" workers receive as much for the few hours they worked as those who had worked all day, we suddenly meet an employer different from any we have ever met.

9. Remember that parables are theological in nature.

One of the most remarkable aspects of Jesus' parables is the way they speak of God. Although parables are thoroughly theological, they make no attempt to describe God's attributes. Instead, the parables lead us into an encounter within the polarity of intimacy and threat of God. The concrete reference points of shepherd, king, father, a woman who sweeps her house, or a vineyard keeper gives us an awareness of God and God's living reality.

Steps in Developing the Homiletical Text

In the process of examining a parable, there are important consider-ations one should note as the study proceeds through the homileti-cal outline and the final draft. These steps will assist the preacher in avoiding the danger of presupposing what the text says and the consequent application in the sermon.[4]

Step #1. *Set aside presumptions about the story and its meaning.* We are vulnerable to misconceptions about Jesus' parables because they tend to be the most familiar of the New Testament stories. We remember their oft telling in Sunday school, hymns, and sermons, which leads to the assumption that we know their deepest and most important lessons. Robert Farrar Capon notes:

> Despite our illusions of understanding [Jesus] better than his first hearers did, we vindicate his chosen method by misnaming—and thus misunderstanding—even the most beloved and familiar par-ables. The Prodigal Son, for example, is not about a boy's vices, it is about a father's forgiveness. The Laborers in the Vineyard are by no means the central character in the story; they are hardly more than stick-figures used by Jesus to rub his hearers' noses in the outrageous grace of a vineyard owner who gives equal pay for unequal work. (Capon 1985, 27)

Step #2. *Take care in reading the text.* As with Step #1, we assume that because we have read the text many times and even preached from it, we know the parable well. Return to the original language. While one need not be fluent in Greek, it is helpful to examine key words as to their various meanings. In the Parable of the Prodigal Son, the younger son, in planning his speech to his father, asks that his father make him into a hired man and not a slave or house worker. The specifics of his request only become apparent in the original language.

Step #3. *Carefully examine the plot, looking for parallel thoughts or words.* What is central and how do the ideas or characters link up? Bailey is particularly helpful here. For example, in the Parable of the Lost Sheep (Luke 15:4-7), the first and third stanzas are "seman-tically related" while the second stanza uses a "poetic device" that assists in understanding the key phrase (Bailey, *Poet and Peasant*, 144).

A Suppose one of you has a hundred sheep

B and loses one of them.

C Does he not leave the ninety-nine in the open country

    1 and go after the lost sheep

        2 until he finds it? And when he finds it,

            3 he joyfully puts it on his shoulders

                4 and goes home. Then he calls his friends and neighbors together and

            3¹ says, 'Rejoice with me;

        2¹ I have found

    1¹ my lost sheep.'

A¹ I tell you that in the same way there will be more rejoicing in heaven

B¹ over one sinner who repents

C¹ than over ninety-nine righteous persons who do not need to repent. [NIV]

Step #4. *Look for the main point of comparison or a cluster of comparisons*, as in the Parable of the Persistent Widow, in which the widow takes on the unjust judge (Luke 18:1-8). While the widow clearly is the one on whom we might first focus our attention, Jesus spends time on the judge. Even though the judge is unjust, Jesus lets us know that by the persistence of the widow the judge will do what is right. But he does not leave us with that thought; he asks, "And will not God bring about justice for his chosen ones, who cry out to him day and night? Will he keep putting them off? I tell you, he will see that they get justice, and quickly." He then concludes with, "However, when the Son of Man comes, will he find faith on the earth?" [NIV]. Michael Ball asks, could it be that "if the judge cannot afford to let a widow besmirch his reputation by having the woman spread around his failure to right her wrong, how much more must God guard his 'name' or his reputation?" (Ball, 100).

Step #5. *Watch for the unexpected.* An important aspect of a parable's nature is the element of surprise. It was Jesus' use of "the Samaritan" that brought a gasp to the hearers. They assumed the good man would be one they could all applaud. The very name "Samaritan" would have been the furthest possibility as those listening tried to guess the rest of the story.

Step #6. *Be observant of detail, especially details that may mean little to us some two thousand years later.* Check out cultural nuances researched by a scholar, for it is often within those details that we find insights that give life and energy to the sermon. In the Good Samaritan, the story takes place between two important cities that provide its framework: Jerusalem, the city of worship, from which the Priest and Levite are coming, and Jericho, the city cursed by Joshua but the suburb in which those religious servants resided between the days of duty in the Temple. As they left the place of worship, they forgot that the very nature of faith was not to be left behind but to be carried into life.

Also, the amount owed by the slave in the Parable of the Unforgiving Slave (Matt. 18:23-35) is so enormous as to stretch credulity to the breaking point. In today's terms it is in the billions of dollars. In preaching this text, if the amount owed were not noted, the humor or hyperbole Jesus used would be missed, leading to the possible misunderstanding of the parable altogether.

So much of our understanding of the Bible is shaped by literature of today and past centuries, such as in the romanticizing of the shepherd. In first-century Palestine, such a person was on a lower rung of the social ladder. The shepherd looking for the lost sheep is not a person whom people of that day would want to associate with the king of Israel! Even their literature made clear how shepherds were to be regarded:

> A man should not teach his son to be an ass-driver or a camel-driver, or a barber or a sailor, or a herdsman[5] or a shopkeeper, for their craft is the craft of robbers. (*m. Qidd.* 4.14)

Step #7. *Note that the Hebrew Scriptures were the only Bible Jesus had to read and the only Scripture with which his hearers would be familiar.* In studying Jesus' parables, look for connections to the Old Testament. Though there are few direct references to Old Testament texts,[6] the entire world of Jesus' experience was based on an Old Testament theological understanding and the ways of God with this people of Israel. This was the religious and cultural foundation of Jesus' theology and history.

Step #8. *Look for other connections in the Synoptic Gospels.* It seems evident that Mark was the first to write, and Matthew and Luke derive much of their material from him. Look to see how they line up with each other, how each one treats a parable, and where he locates it within the text. The Matthew (25:14-30) and Luke (19:12-27) treatments of the "talents" need to be examined in the preaching of either text.

The task of the preacher is to take what Jesus said and translate that into a contemporary understanding and application. We do not have Jesus around to ask about what he meant but we do have the Gospels, which were the basis on which the church was built. Taking care to understand Jesus' stories as would first-century Palestinian Jews, we examine them as unique tools in the mouth of Jesus to convey eternal principles of God, helping us believe and follow.

Preaching Parables to a Postmodern Age

The shift from modernity to postmodernity requires preachers to consider different ways to reach those of the postmodern culture. We can better see today the transition in the Western world from a mind-set shaped by the age of reason and its associated themes to an age increasingly shaped by ideas grouped under the category of postmodernity.

We've also seen how parables are uniquely adept at attracting and speaking into minds and hearts influenced by those themes and ideas of postmodernity. While parables are only one genre of preaching material, they do provide an effective means of circumventing many of the points of resistance of the postmodern age, assisting the preacher in making clear the great themes of the teaching of Jesus. This is not to say that preaching should avoid confronting and challenging postmodern thought. Biblical preaching ought to challenge ideas that set themselves up in opposition to the reign of Christ. However, here we are examining how parables can effectively speak into the postmodern situation through windows opened by these shifting patterns of thought.

In summary, there are a number of ways in which you will find the preaching of parables is particularly effective in reaching the postmodern age. This is not to say that Jesus' parables are universal and timeless only to a postmodern world. However, there is a remarkable convergence between postmodern thought and the parables of Jesus. This is what tends to make the use of parables a particularly helpful entry point for the preaching task for this postmodern age. There are seven ways in which preaching the parables can serve to speak the gospel into this contemporary mind.

1. The postmodern rejection of reason as the only sure way to discover truth also rejects teaching that disconnects mind from heart and invites discovery by way of intuition and experience. This longing can be spoken to, for example, through the Parable of the Pharisee and Tax Collector (Luke 18:9-14). In this parable Jesus exposes the falsity of faith based on keeping rules by voicing his objection to religious belief trapped by rigid categories. While this parable does not give room for faith located outside the framework of a knowable and present God, it doesn't require the hearer to believe God before the lesson of the parable can be understood. Jesus applauds the tax collector for his faith even while despised by his countrymen. He also points out how being humble in coming to God invites forgiveness.

This parable is an example of Jesus' invitation for people to come in faith. Their acceptance into his household of faith is not because of what they know or how good they live but by their honesty in asking and receiving God's forgiveness.

2. The postmodern rejection of truth as being objective and its corollary that "truth" is relative challenge the gospel and its truth claims. Parables provide a means of speaking in such a way that one does not have to confront this assumption immediately or directly. Instead, the preacher is able to invite the postmodern—anxious over Jesus' claim to the "truth"—to examine his or her life.

For example, in the Parable of the Sower (Matt. 13:1-23), the focus is on the role of the learner. Each of the four soils "chooses" whether or not the seed will live and reproduce or if it will die. In this parable, there is not an overpowering God who insists that the "soil" accepts his truth claim. Instead, the burden of responsibility is reversed.

The power of this parable is to induce an inquisitive response: The hearers will never know if the seed is truth until they become hospitable and choose to be a recipient of the seed. Hospitality is their choice. They decide whether or not they invite the seed or hold the kingdom-claim at arm's length. If they reject it, however, they will never know if the seed is indeed the coming kingdom.

In light of the postmodern reluctance to believe in truth as objective, parables invite people to test Jesus and discover whether or not his claim to truth has validity for their lives.

3. The rejection of authority as "expressions and masks of the primal will to power" (Veith, 158) leads in postmodern thought to seeing history as a distortion, written by those who wield power. Therefore, all institutions and relationships—including political and institutional—are in essence a will to power. While parables were not given by Jesus to refute today's postmodern conclusions necessarily, they do address many issues that concern postmoderns, including the matter of power.

For example, the Parable of the Persistent Widow/Unjust Judge (Luke 18:1-8) invites the listener to feel the distress of the marginalized woman who, without husband or defender, strikes out in earnest to pry a judge out of his self-serving conduct and mete out fairness and justice. The parable gives no time for a lament on her predicament or a judgment of those responsible for her being a victim. The story does alert the listener to the abuse by the powerful and to her vulnerability, which Jesus acknowledges. But he also makes it clear how much God—even though represented by a miserable judge—wants to come alongside and aid those crushed by the powerful. What Jesus doesn't do is fall prey to doing for the widow what she must do for herself. "Yes, this world is run by the powerful," Jesus seems to be acknowledging, "but even so, God is willing to fight alongside those who, in their predicament, continue to press God for an answer to their need."

To the postmodern view of power, this parable provides an example of God's concern in rewriting the stories of those in need.

4. Postmodern thinking not only rejects truth as objective but also rejects that one can write a story—metanarrative—for all people. Thus the Bible, in particular, is discounted for its wider story, which begins at creation, describes the fall and the demoralizing events caused by the human will, and ends in a wrap-up of history. This postmodern discounting of a metanarrative strikes at the very core of biblical faith. Nothing seems more basic in understanding Jesus than to know within the story of our fall and rise how much the human race is in need of a savior. It is here that parables provide a helpful way, however. They insert smaller stories that contain seeds of the larger story.

For example, in the Parable of the Prodigal Son (Luke 15:1-32) the framework for the larger narrative is germane to the story of the relationship of the two sons to their father. But one does not have to preach that. The remarkable love of the father, in which he chooses to embarrass himself so as to protect his son from humiliation, describes God's fatherly love. The story can be seen as a story of an earthly father's love or it can be seen as describing God. The choice is up to the person listening.

To the postmodern denial of the grand story, parables don't begin with the wider landscape but instead begin on the ground where people live. So, in this parable, a loving parent becomes the introduction to the grand story of God's love. As a story, it has appeal to the postmodern worldview that rejects the larger story for people of all situations. With the postmodern rejection of the metanarrative as the wider explanation of life, the mini-narrative becomes less offensive or threatening.

Parables locate Jesus' message within a story and by so doing appeal to the intuitive and experiential nature of the postmodern.

5. Reacting to the modernist view that identity is found in the autonomy of the individual, postmodernity instead sees identity within the collective and community. This is not foreign to Jesus' vision of the kingdom. For example, in the Parable of the Rich Fool (Luke 12:13-34) Jesus tells a story in response to a question from a young man who wants Jesus to settle an inheritance issue he is having with his brother. Jesus responds to this request with a parable, in which he describes a rich man who is foolish because he fails to integrate wealth with wisdom: He lacks wisdom in that he spends his wealth without respect for others. In this story Jesus gives us his view of what is going on in the young man's—the one who asked the question in the first place—life. Jesus interprets his problem as greed triumphing over a relationship with his brother. And for Jesus, wisdom is expressed in our choice to live within relationships.

This postmodern view of refocusing human identity within the community—when seen in balance—fits within Jesus' message. Jesus provides a helpful example of how he, too, sees people within the important context of relationships. Not only does this parable support the vital importance of community, but it does so within his wider vision of the people of God living in relationship to each other and to him.

6. Postmodernity judges the contemporary world as being culturally conditioned and views language as a prison. While preaching will from time to time challenge culturally driven (mis)conceptions, its foremost call is to advance the teachings and life of Jesus. However, the gospel does acknowledge that while language is the very means by which we come to truth, it also can become links in the chains of bondage. For example, the Parable of the Good Samaritan (Luke 10:25-37) exposes the cultural bondage of the Priest and Levite who are unwilling—or maybe culturally unable—to move outside their defined roles: Expectations driven by their roles kept them from (at least, in this story) doing good. The name "Samaritan" so triggered antagonism as to prevent the lawyer, in the end, from even saying the word "Samaritan." Jesus, by way of this parable, acknowledges that language can be defeating.

One way to circumnavigate the shoals of postmodern sensibilities is to allow stories to show how God breaks through cultural concerns and frees people from cultural bondage.

7. A hallmark of the modern era was optimism, fueled by a belief in the inevitability of progress. For the postmodern, the opposite is true: Progress is not inevitable. This, alongside rejecting metanarrative, ends up in the discounting of a historical—or eschatological—vision of God. So how does the preacher unfold an understanding of the transcendent God who is the beginning and ending, the first and the last, and whose creation has purpose and destiny?

Parables provide an out-of-the-box way of thinking, inviting the listener to look in new ways at an issue. This inductive approach invites the hearer to walk around to the other side of the issue and ask, "What does it look like from here?"

Regarding the postmodern rejection of the inevitability of human progress, Jesus, in the Parable of the Friend at Midnight (Luke 11:1-13), describes a person with a severe problem: He has no bread to serve a friend who has come at midnight. What is he to do? Admit his problem and let the matter die, along with his reputation, or seek out an answer and, by so doing, move from dilemma to solution? In this case, progress is not inevitable. The solution is only found as the person in need seeks a solution.

The heart of the story lies in the determination to find a solution. In that sense, the solution or moving forward is not inevitable. It requires "chutzpah": He is called on to intercede with his neighbor.

The ingenious characteristic of this parable is that it invites the postmodern to discover that God wants to help in solving issues and to provide for God's people by moving them past roadblocks.

~

The form of public speaking perfected in first-century Palestine by Jesus offers a way of speaking into the mind/heart of a person of the twenty-first century. Image-driven and story-taught, these current generations not only have enormous experience in operating within stories, they know how to exegete, making sense of what is said by way of image and metaphor, applying to life the lessons taught.

For all generations, the parabolic form has been a powerful tool in communicating the message of Jesus to any culture and people. Today it has increased suitability. The postmodern mind is remarkably open to this form of thinking about life. This, in the end, is biblical preaching, even if hearers may not think of it that way.

In any age to any people, preaching the gospel requires careful exegeting of both the audience and the text. Preaching parables is not the only way to preach to a postmodern. However, as a story it has an appeal to a worldview that rejects the larger story of life but is open, indeed curious, about the smaller stories. The preacher looks for ways to seed the Word. The use of parables is such a way.

The parabolic form is like a stealth bomber, sweeping undetected under the radar of postmodern angst, yet able to deliver that which is biblical and Christ-centered.

3

A Study of Parables
for Sermon Preparation

Now that we have looked at the nature of the postmodern mind and examined the nature of the parables of Jesus, it is time to begin the preparation of the sermon. Here we will look at ten parables. The scholars I reference here are from a rather wide variety; however, being evangelical and therefore bringing such assumptions to the preaching tasks, I tend to spend more time with evangelical scholars. Nevertheless, one must always be willing to push out to wider fields in the search for the very best of biblical scholarship in building the sermon.

In the process of examining a parable, I approach each study in a particular way, which I explain below, so as to understand it before I begin the actual sermon writing. What I've wanted to do for you as a preacher is to examine the very best of scholars and bring to you what you may need as a basic resource in preaching from any one of these ten parables. My choice of these parables is based on finding a representative selection as a way of using the various windows of postmodernity as entry points to our people and culture.

First, let me tell you how and why I treat the study of each parable, and then I'll use that pattern or template to work on each of the parables.

Text

Unless otherwise noted, the biblical translation that I offer and reference in the study is the New International Version.

This parable's unique window

Here I write a brief description of the window the parable provides as an opening for ministry into a contemporary, postmodern world.

Position of the parable within the text

Where the writers of the Gospel place the parable is important in understanding the word pictures created within the parable. Where it is within the wider text—what precedes and follows the parable, people linked to the parable by way of an opening question or interaction with Jesus—may provide clues to its meaning.

Word study

Some of the parables include words that require special analysis: The English translation may be less than adequate, or a particular word may have a special meaning to the people of that day.

Cultural factors

Because context is essential to understanding Jesus' parables, it is critical to examine social and political realities that cradled his message. The challenge is to understand these stories within the first-century Middle Eastern culture rather than see them through the lens and ambiance of the twenty-first-century Western world. To get at the heart of the parables, the cultural factors that bear upon the interpretation are studied.

Subject

Stating the subject makes it clear what topic the parable is addressing. Usually this is framed within a question. This requires that in the study of the parable (or any text) one must unearth the central issue at which the story or paragraph is driving. This discipline is so important because it provides the anchor from which one's musing and sermonizing is held. It is an important device as a reminder in the sermon of what we want, at the end, our people to understand.

Complement

The complement states what the parable says about the subject. Here one writes out in what ways the parable brings forth the supporting material to make the subject substantive. You will see when we get to the actual parable how this provides, along with the subject, a reminder at all stages in the sermon preparation and delivery of what the text is saying.

The surprise

Each parable contains a surprise, a turn in the road, an unexpected resolution, something that would have elicited an "ah" from the listener. Often the surprise is the device Jesus used to drive home the message of the parable. For listeners some two thousand years later, the challenge is to pick up on the culturally nuanced factors underscoring the parables, without which the basic insights of the parables would be missed.

Exegetical outline

It is better to do an exegetical outline of the text before you move on to writing the homiletical outline. The exegetical outline is making out what the text is saying. When you get to the homiletical outline, that is the stage at which you move from what the text says to what the text is saying to your congregation today. So, exercise the discipline of making sense of what the text is saying itself before you jump into the next stage.

Homiletical outline

Once the exegetical outline is finished and you are satisfied that you have a good grasp of what the text is saying, then move on to bringing the text into today's world. Here you want to ask, What then might the Spirit have the text say to my people this week? You are now at the place where you examine the text with respect to how it might be treated in a sermon.

The big idea

The structure of the sermon is framed around "the big idea" of the sermon (see Robinson, 31–44). "The big idea" informs the listeners what is central to the parable and essential to the lessons applied. Often, however, preachers assume a three-point sermon is essential to good preaching. We make the mistake of assuming the Bible works best when using this logical sequence. The value of "the big idea" approach is to build in the mind of the listener an understanding of the most essential point the text is making and how that applies to living on Monday.

Here is a question we need to ask ourselves: "When members of the congregation leave the service, what is remembered?" The chances are unlikely they will recall in twenty-four hours (or even in one hour) the logical sequence of our carefully worked out three- or four-point sermon. The reason for shaping the sermon around the central idea of the text is that it helps the preacher develop the sermon to focus on what above all else the text is saying and ensure the sermon resonates in the heart of the hearer throughout the week.

Material in order of the text

Here I examine the material with a verse-by-verse study of the text.

Homiletical considerations

After the above has been completed, then you want to see what special considerations you need to be giving this parable out of the issues and problems it surfaces. This is helpful as you research for complementary material and then move toward the actual writing of the sermon.

Parable One: The Sower (Matthew 13:1-23)

There are three texts on the Sower: Matthew 13:1-23; Mark 4:1-9; and Luke 8:4-8. This study comes from Matthew's text.

Text

¹That same day Jesus went out of the house and sat by the lake. ²Such large crowds gathered around him that he got into a boat and sat in it, while all the people stood on the shore. ³Then he told them many things in parables, saying: "A farmer went out to sow his seed. ⁴As he was scattering the seed, some fell along the path, and the birds came and ate it up. ⁵Some fell on rocky places, where it did not have much soil. It sprang up quickly, because the soil was shallow. ⁶But when the sun came up, the plants were scorched, and they withered because they had no root. ⁷Other seed fell among thorns, which grew up and choked the plants. ⁸Still other seed fell on good soil, where it produced a crop—a

hundred, sixty or thirty times what was sown. [9]He who has ears, let him hear."

[10]The disciples came to him and asked, "Why do you speak to the people in parables?"

[11]He replied, "The knowledge of the secrets of the kingdom of heaven has been given to you, but not to them. [12]Whoever has will be given more, and he will have an abundance. Whoever does not have, even what he has will be taken from him. [13]This is why I speak to them in parables:

"Though seeing, they do not see;
   though hearing, they do not hear or understand.

[14]In them is fulfilled the prophecy of Isaiah:

"'You will be ever hearing but never understanding;
   you will be ever seeing but never perceiving.

[15]For this people's heart has become calloused;
   they hardly hear with their ears,
   and they have closed their eyes.
Otherwise they might see with their eyes,
   hear with their ears,
   understand with their hearts
   and turn, and I would heal them.'

[16]But blessed are your eyes because they see, and your ears because they hear. [17]For I tell you the truth, many prophets and righteous men longed to see what you see but did not see it, and to hear what you hear but did not hear it.

[18]"Listen then to what the parable of the sower means: [19]When anyone hears the message about the kingdom and does not understand it, the evil one comes and snatches away what was sown in his heart. This is the seed sown along the path. [20]The one who received the seed that fell on rocky places is the man who hears the word and at once receives it with joy. [21]But since he has no root, he lasts only a short time. When trouble or persecution comes because of the word, he quickly falls away. [22]The one who received the seed that fell among the thorns is the man who hears the word, but the worries of this life and the deceitfulness of wealth choke it, making it unfruitful. [23]But the one who received the seed that fell on good soil is the man who hears the word and understands it. He produces a crop, yielding a hundred, sixty or thirty times what was sown."

This parable's unique preaching window to postmoderns

This parable confronts rather than seduces a postmodern mind. While there is no picture of God bursting in with greatness and wisdom, the use of "soil"—a metaphor of minds and hearts—makes it clear that the hearer is responsible for understanding his message. Jesus is quite pointed in his challenge: If you don't get the message you will be judged. Responsibility for being receptive to his kingdom is put on the hearer, a rather shocking wake-up call for the listener.

Position of the parable within the text

While the focus of this parable is on the soil that receives the seed, within the context of the text Jesus speaks to the multitudes, which may imply that the task of spreading the seed is not just for his disciples but for everyone.

What is unusual here is that Jesus gives his own homily. When a storyteller concludes the story with his interpretation of its meaning, it is a signal to take it seriously. Jesus then follows up the parable with a call for decision, something quite different from rabbinic parables, which were more a means to reinforce an Old Testament principle or text.

In Matthew's prelude (12:46-50), Jesus warns that his call supersedes one's loyalty to family, a bold claim out of step with Middle Eastern family ties. By so doing he places over the entire text an assertion of the gospel's domain in all of life.

Evident in this text are the many struggles Jesus had in getting the teachers of the law to understand the nature of his kingdom:

a. The Pharisees accuse his disciples of violating the Sabbatarian laws by eating grain as they walk through the fields (12:1-14).
b. When the Pharisees charge Jesus with being "Beelzebub, the prince of demons," he challenges their understanding, pointing out their ignorance and the inconsistency of their logic (12:22-37).
c. In response to the Pharisees' request that he perform a miracle, he gives them the three-day sign of Jonah (12:38-45).

Increasingly common in the life of Jesus is his popularity with the people. His direct and illustrative messages, his warnings of coming difficulty, his linkage with John the Baptist, the authority of his teachings—so unlike others the people heard—along with his healings and miracles created something of a pop-hero frenzy (Jones, 65).

Word study

Kingdom. Between the parable and the homily, Jesus links the story to Isaiah's reference to the coming kingdom (13:14-15). While at first this may seem discriminatory against those who fail to understand Jesus' sayings, it is not a double cross. Jesus is not going out of his way to trick people. However, you can almost see Jesus shaking his head at the obtuseness of people, saying, "You are what Isaiah was speaking about when he said, 'Though seeing, they do not see; though hearing, they do not hear or understand.'" Jesus' inclusion of Isaiah is not parenthetical; he wants the disciples to get his meaning.

The evangelists, in writing their Gospels later—after Jesus' death and resurrection—saw their misunderstanding of Jesus' comments on his coming death. One might suppose that if his own disciples could not make sense of his parables, or if the Pharisees could not recognize that they were examples of the hard soil, how could they expect the casual listener to understand?

Soil. Jesus identifies four types of soil and how the seed fared: On hardened pathways the seed was *devoured* by birds; on rocky soil the seed was *scorched*; among the thorns the seed was *choked*; and in good soil the seed brought a great *yield*.

Farmers of that day carefully used all available soil for planting. While pathways wound their way between the fields so as not to affect the important sowing areas, they became hardened. This hardening made it easier, then, for birds to locate the fallen seed. Because limestone lay just under the shallow surface of soil, much of the land lacked sufficient topsoil to cover the seed adequately, making it vulnerable to the heat of the day. Seed sown in soil dominated by thorns and weeds had to fight for sunlight and nutrients. Good soil provided both nutrients for germinating the seed and sufficient space for growing.

Seeds. Seeds are small in comparison to what they produce. When dropped into soil, it is not self-evident that anything will ever appear. As a seed begins its life journey it can not be seen; it is obscured and lost and, in effect, dies as the outer skin rots and falls off. Its mystery is that it comes to life only after it "dies."

The Sower. Who is the sower? Is it God or is everyone who follows Jesus a sower? Nothing within the three Gospel renditions suggests that Jesus saw himself as the only sower. While it is obvious here that he is the one sowing, his invitation for all to engage in his enterprise is explicit. In effect, everyone who follows Jesus is to be a part of spreading his good news.

There is a question concerning the sower's competence: Given the high cost of seed grain, why did this farmer not take better care to prevent the seed from falling in places he knew were unproductive? Given that a Middle Eastern farmer knew his fields from years of careful tending, why does he allow the seed to fall on the road, on thin soil, and among weeds?

There are two explanations. First, the sower does not sow equally in each of these four quadrants: The farmer would exercise great care to ensure that the seed was maximized, with little of it falling anywhere other than where good soil is located. Some seed, however, would occasionally fall on the first three types of soil.

Second, this is a parable and the focus is not on the sower. In describing the types of soil inhospitable to the good news, Jesus is simply using this to shape his story.

A characteristic of Jesus' parables is inclusivity: There is a universality about his stories in that his characters seem to represent all of us, or the circumstances he describes fit into one's own experience. Listeners will see themselves in the characters, the situations he describes, and the problems he creates: They are real life.

Cultural factors

Political Expectations of the Messiah. Jesus confused everyone. He announced his kingdom to a people driven into the ground by the overwhelming presence of the Romans. Expectations were riding high. When Jesus arrived on the scene, the deep river of messianic hope was fed by two powerful currents, both wanting to secure national independence and stability. The Zealots, a Jewish party trumpeting a radical nationalism, were ready for war and were game to try to overthrow the Romans. Their deepening anger against the Romans was heightened by what they regarded as an unholy alliance between religious leaders and Rome.

People were looking for one who would deal with these factions and restore peace to their land. They were not only surprised but disappointed. Jesus did not pick up the sword to drive out the Romans, nor did he accept the public celebration on Palm Sunday and take possession of David's throne. His talk about power and authority concerned itself with the rule of one's own spirit. They were confused. There was no announcement of the overthrow of Rome.

In his talks about the kingdom, it must have seemed bizarre to them for Jesus to imply that his kingdom was like David's—indeed, its very fulfillment—and then to come up with a farm example of seed as the way to understand his kingdom. It was like promising to develop a winning hockey team by teaching knitting.

But even if they had come to understand Jesus' message, such a frail embodiment of life as a small seed was so far from what they thought was needed to defeat evil as to make it absurd. If Satan was to be defeated, God would need to launch a more formidable program than farming. Undoubtedly, the disciples might have wondered, "What in the world does he mean by this kind of story when what we need is a strategy to defeat the evil one and run the Romans out of town?"

Farming. Farming was more than just a vocation or way of life; it was the backbone of the economy and the prime means of existence. Middle Easterners knew crop failure resulted in starvation. That is why they understood the nature and aspects of soil. Understanding where to sow was life itself: To sow on paths, rocky soil, and among weeds was foolish. Seed was just too precious (Young, 251–58). So, what kind of crazy storyteller was this?

Yield. Could seed bring a yield of thirty-, sixty-, or a hundredfold? Thirtyfold was astounding. Sixty was unheard of, but a hundred was off the charts! The percentage yield is not the issue, however, as Jesus' use of hyperbole helps him make his point (Hultgren, 187–88). As well, a "hundredfold" could have been seen as a sign of blessing—as with Isaac's crop yielding a hundredfold—signifying an extraordinary blessing of God (Gen. 26:12) (see Scott 1989, 355–58).

Subject
How does God's kingdom take hold of the world?

Complement

The kingdom of God takes hold as people become hearers through whom God spreads the divine life.

The surprise

This parable lacks a strong element of surprise, unlike most parables. New Testament scholar Charles Hedrick does wonder why there is no mention of plowing (Hedrick, 172). If the farmer had first plowed the land before sowing—as would be normally the case—would that have made a difference? An interesting question, but hardly important to its understanding. The setting simply creates the landscape for the message with details serving the message, not the other way around.

Exegetical outline

This exegesis includes both the parable (13:3-8) and Jesus' homily (13:19-23).
  I.   The sower goes to the field to spread the seed (v. 3b).
       A. The sower well knows the process required to bring a harvest.
       B. The sower also understands what is needed for the seed to reproduce.
       C. The sower knows that the seed he sows will reproduce.
  II. Jesus describes three types of soil that result in failure (vv. 4-7).
       A. The hard ground is where birds feed, picking up the seed.
       B. The rocky ground does not allow the seed to root.
       C. The thorny ground snuffs out the seed's ability to find nutrients.
  III. Jesus points out soil in which the seed grows and reproduces successfully (v. 8).
       A. In the good soil the seed reproduces an enormous crop.
       B. Jesus concludes with a reminder that only those who really listen will understand.

Homiletical outline

  I.   Growing the kingdom requires people who believe in its importance.

A. Kingdom builders know what is required to bring a kingdom harvest.
B. People engaged in growing the kingdom believe in the nature and power of the seed.
C. Kingdom people also know what seed will produce.

II. Just because we do the work of God does not mean we are always successful.
A. Sometimes the seed of God's Word drops in places where it is wasted.
B. Some people are superficial, so what they learn about God lasts a day or so and then dies.
C. Spreading Christ's news means we have to compete with other distractions that can snuff out the life of the gospel.

III. There are some who are ready and anxious to hear and believe the good news.
A. There is an enormous potential as the seed of God is received with faith.
B. Jesus reminds us, however, that the receiving of God's kingdom comes about as people are open to hearing the gospel.

The big idea

Trust God and spread the gospel; spread the gospel and trust God.

Material in order of the text

Unique to this parable is that Jesus follows it up with an explanation to the disciples as to its meaning. Thus, preaching this parable requires linking the parable with the homily (vv. 3-8).

> [3]Then he told them many things in parables, saying: "A farmer went out to sow his seed. [4]As he was scattering the seed, some fell along the path, and the birds came and ate it up. . . ."
> [18]"Listen then to what the parable of the sower means: [19]When anyone hears the message about the kingdom and does not understand it, the evil one comes and snatches away what was sown in his heart. This is the seed sown along the path."

The seed along the path has no chance of survival. It is not as if the farmer did not try to keep the seed from falling where the birds could pick it up. No farmer can guarantee that 100 percent of the seed will land in favorable places. Fields in Palestine were small, separated by footpaths. As the sower walked the field, some seed would fall on hardened paths where birds would more readily pick it up.

People's lives become resistant as they choose familiar cultural paths often hardened to the gospel. When the seed of faith falls on worn paths, the hardened soil leaves it vulnerable to "birds" searching for food.

> [5]"Some fell on rocky places, where it did not have much soil. It sprang up quickly, because the soil was shallow. [6]But when the sun came up, the plants were scorched, and they withered because they had no root...."
>
> [20]"The one who received the seed that fell on rocky places is the man who hears the word and at once receives it with joy. [21]But since he has no root, he lasts only a short time. When trouble or persecution comes because of the word, he quickly falls away."

As seed germinates in the thin layer of soil, there is little soil in which it can grow, symbolic of the hearer who at first is enthusiastic, but as troubles come or the realization of commitment dawns, enthusiasm shrivels. With insufficient soil to grow roots, the young plant, unable to withstand the hot and dry sun, withers.

> [7]"Other seed fell among thorns, which grew up and choked the plants...."
>
> [22]"The one who received the seed that fell among the thorns is the man who hears the word, but the worries of this life and the deceitfulness of wealth choke it, making it unfruitful."

This soil represents people preoccupied with
a.   the worries of life,
b.   the deceitfulness of wealth.
It is not that this kind of soil is unable to provide the nutrients for growth but that the seed is forced to compete with the surrounding weeds. Luke records,

> "The seed that fell among thorns stands for those who hear, but as they go on their way they are choked by life's worries, riches and pleasures, and they do not mature." (Luke 8:14)

⁸"Still other seed fell on good soil, where it produced a crop—a hundred, sixty, or thirty times what was sown. ⁹He who has ears, let him hear. . . ."

²³"But the one who received the seed that fell on good soil is the man who hears the word and understands it. He produces a crop, yielding a hundred, sixty, or thirty times what was sown."

Jesus' challenge—"He who has ears, let him hear" (Matt. 13:9)—is not unlike "Those who want to hear what I'm saying, listen carefully!" The disciples were agitated that Jesus was not pushing out the Romans and grasping hold of the leadership of Israel—this story was for them. Rather than taking up the sword, Jesus was spreading far and wide his kingly vision—and by implication, the disciples too should see themselves as sowers rather than military commanders.

This is the good soil in which seed explodes to a hundredfold yield. It is "good" because

a. It has been prepared by being plowed and fertilized, working up the soil, and destroying the weeds.
b. The soil breaks down the exterior of the seed so the germ can send out its shoots and begin its journey of growth and reproduction.
c. The soil has sufficient nutrients and moisture to reproduce the seed grain, some thirty, others sixty, and others one hundred times.

Homiletical considerations

1. The challenge of preaching this parable to postmoderns is to move them from their natural desire to be successful, as symbolized by the fourth soil, to understand the larger vision of Christ's kingdom seed. As an entry-level parable, it may not be helpful to attempt to "prove" God. Rather, allow the creative modifier of each soil to either repel—as in the first three soils—or to attract—as in the fourth soil. The concluding lines should then push the hearer to recognize that the onus is on him or her to be that kind of person who is open to receive what is good, for the fourth soil is not a neutral participant in the process.

2. Because this is a farming story, it might be helpful for preachers raised in the city to ask farmers for their analysis.

3. This is not a parable about failure. While some seed grain is lost, the parable does not call us to lament its loss but celebrates the success of the harvest.

4. There are two ways to see this parable:

a.   Focus on the four kinds of soil.

b.   Make the seed central to the story.

5. There are three major movements in this parable; while there is no surprise, there is tension between the idea of the disciples sowing seed and launching a new order. That something as innocuous as seed will upset the world is preposterous.

a.   In the first movement explain why Jesus saw it necessary to explain his coming by using the metaphor of seed.

b.   In the second movement explain the four kinds of soil by way of contemporary examples.

c.   The third movement is the stunning result: up to a hundred-fold!

Parable Two:
The Unforgiving Servant (Matthew 18:21-35)

Text

²¹Then Peter came to Jesus and asked, "Lord, how many times shall I forgive my brother when he sins against me? Up to seven times?"

²²Jesus answered, "I tell you, not seven times, but seventy-seven times.

²³"Therefore, the kingdom of heaven is like a king who wanted to settle accounts with his servants. ²⁴As he began the settlement, a man who owed him ten thousand talents was brought to him. ²⁵Since he was not able to pay, the master ordered that he and his wife and his children and all that he had be sold to repay the debt.

²⁶"The servant fell on his knees before him. 'Be patient with me,' he begged, 'and I will pay back everything.' ²⁷The servant's master took pity on him, canceled the debt and let him go.

²⁸"But when that servant went out, he found one of his fellow servants who owed him a hundred denarii. He grabbed him and began to choke him. 'Pay back what you owe me!' he demanded.

²⁹"His fellow servant fell to his knees and begged him, 'Be patient with me, and I will pay you back.'

³⁰"But he refused. Instead, he went off and had the man thrown into prison until he could pay the debt. ³¹When the other servants saw what had happened, they were greatly distressed and went and told their master everything that had happened.

³²"Then the master called the servant in. 'You wicked servant,' he said, 'I canceled all that debt of yours because you begged me to. ³³Shouldn't you have had mercy on your fellow servant just as I had on you?' ³⁴In anger his master turned him over to the jailers to be tortured, until he should pay back all he owed.

³⁵"This is how my heavenly Father will treat each of you unless you forgive your brother from your heart."

This is a story fit for the stage, with its color, radical shifts in behavior, circumstance, and personalities. It moves the audience from feelings of understanding and empathy to disgust, horror, and revulsion, only to be moved again to see themselves in the one to detest.

This parable's unique preaching window to postmoderns

Ethics is a particularly potent subject in postmodernity. Examples of clergy violation, insider trading, and abuses of genetic research make ethics a high priority. This parable enters into that world of shady and self-serving manipulation. While God is not mentioned, the king with power, like a contemporary CEO, implies a reference to God. The incredible amount owed to the forgiving king makes the first servant into quite a rascal. How he then treats another over whom he also has power and for whom proper ethical behavior matters is critical. In the end, the listeners are brought face-to-face with their own power over others: whether they will forgive or not.

Position of the parable within the text

Earlier in the chapter Jesus, in teaching about his kingdom, uses a child to describe what it requires to enter his kingdom. In a world where children were regarded as being important but ruled within the strictures of a patriarchal world, Jesus stuns his listeners. Not only does he set children as the standard for entrance to his kingdom, he condemns anyone who misleads them into sin. The punishment is not a slap on the wrist but "it would be better for him to have a large millstone hung around his neck and be drowned in the depths of the sea" (Matt. 18: 6b). Surely the standard of entrance would be defined by a teacher of the law and not some messy, unkept child. Not with Jesus. He overturns cultural expectations in this text and the following parables.

In the Parable of the Lost Sheep, the shepherd leaves his ninety-nine to find the one lost. Everything set aside to find the wandering, foolish sheep results in the joy of finding the lost one. Jesus concludes the parable by returning to the example of the child and continues with teaching how to handle a person unwilling to settle a dispute. To those he says, if they refuse, treat them as if they were "a pagan or a tax collector" (Matt. 18:17). Jesus does not exclude "pagans or tax collectors" from his ministry, however; he spends time with them, he argues in their defense and offers them forgiveness, the opposite of what this verse seems to suggest. What Jesus is doing is arguing the opposite. To use a metaphor from boxing, he delivers a sucker punch: As they think he is moving one way, he shifts to the other foot and delivers the knockout punch.

This parable provides a framework on how to deal with those who have sinned against us. It is within this question that Jesus delivers a comprehensive absolute: "Whatever you bind on earth will be bound in heaven, and whatever you loose on earth will be loosed in heaven" (v. 18). How frightful the responsibility! How awesome is the power given to his people. Then it becomes evident what he means: Such power is not to be used by those who think they are without sin, but by those who are filled with grace.

It is not evident at first how verses 21-22 connect to forgiving "seventy times seven."[1] Robert Farrar Capon makes the connection: "I take them to mean that if two of Jesus' disciples—if, that is, his followers in their plural capacity as his witnessing church—agree to forgive rather than to excommunicate, then the Father will ratify and confirm their decision with all the power of his grace. And he will do that precisely because wherever two or three are gathered together in Jesus' name (that is, wherever the witnessing church is), there is Jesus himself, the friend of publicans and sinners, the Good Shepherd who lays down his life for the sheep, the beloved Son in whom the Father sees his whole creation forgiven and made new" (Capon 1988, 45).

Word study

Ten Thousand Talents. The amount is staggering.[2] One talent equaled six thousand denarii, and a single denarius equaled roughly a day's income. In today's economy—for an average wage earner—the debt of 10,000 talents is roughly equivalent to $9 billion.

This amount is so outside the realm of possibility that the audience would know Jesus was exaggerating to make his point: His people are in such debt to the Creator that it defies description.

Daneion. "Debt" is better translated as "loan."

Cultural factors

Kings. A "king" in the Middle East obtained his position through intrigue and power struggles. He would keep his power not through democratic means or fair play of the marketplace, but by ruthless exercise of power, stopping at no lengths to consolidate his power and wealth. The ruling assumption, then, was that he could plunder at will, standing above the law and beyond restraints (Herzog, 136).

To rule, a king needed trusted bureaucrats to run his daily enterprise. There were three levels: The lowest were the *illiterati*, including porters and jailers; the *literati*, or scribes, lawyers, and accountants; and the highest, *dignitates*, or those in charge of the largest bureaucratic agencies. Within these levels, intrigue and power plays were at work, as those at the lowest levels attempted to move up and those at the top sought to entrench their power. To protect himself, a king would often change the positions of the *dignitates* so as to manage the inevitable corruption. The *literati* (record keepers) knew what was going on, as they were responsible for the details. This parable deals with people on the top two levels. "It was a cutthroat world constructed around competing pyramids of patron-client loyalties" (Herzog, 137).

The bureaucracies were divided into military, administrative, financial, and ideological (religious) areas. The primary task of those in the financial area was to collect tribute money from conquered peoples and taxation from their own people.

The kings—mostly Gentiles—farmed out the job of collecting taxes to the highest bidder, with the assumption that the winning bidder could skim off the top by adding on tax. In this parable, at accounting time the servant was not able to pay for his bid.

This parable seems somewhat overblown on how the average citizen would have seen his or her king or ruler. The Jews of this period were most acquainted with rulers—apart from Pilate who ruled directly from Rome in Judea—such as the Hasmonean and Herodian kings, who ruled much like their Roman counterparts. They would have linked "kings" with harsh rulers who demanded high taxes and tribute.

Subject
How can we give unlimited forgiveness?

Complement
We are to forgive as Jesus did.

The surprise
The huge debt owed by the first servant ($9 billion) compared to the smaller amount owed by the second servant (about $40,000, or an average worker's annual income) is, by comparison, next to nothing.

Exegetical outline
I.   Peter and Jesus have a conversation that forgiveness is to be unlimited (vv. 21-22).
II. Jesus answers the question, "How can a person extend unlimited forgiveness?" (vv. 23-27).
   A.   The king orders the servant's family and assets sold in payment of the debt.
   B.   The servant begs for time to repay.
   C.   The king takes the debt on himself and pays it.
III. The forgiven servant confronts one of his own debtors (vv. 28-31).
   A.   He insists that the debt be paid immediately.
   B.   The debtor pleads for time.
   C.   The servant refuses and throws his debtor in prison.
   D.   Other servants go to the king with the story.
IV. The king faces his forgiven servant (vv. 32-34).
   A.   He wonders why his forgiven servant did not forgive his debtor.
   B.   He throws the servant in jail.
V.   Jesus gives a closing comment on the nature of forgiveness (v. 35).

Homiletical outline

I. How is it possible to give unlimited forgiveness?
    A. Our debt of sin is more than the sum total of our sins.
    B. The nature of that forgiveness is total and without remainder.
    C. We cannot earn our way out from under the load of debt.
II. We can forgive an unlimited number of times because we have been forgiven.
    A. By seeing how we have been forgiven, we see how vital it is to forgive others.
    B. We struggle to forgive others their misdeeds to us.
    C. There is liberation in learning to forgive.

The big idea

Because we have been forgiven, Christ calls us to forgive others.

Material in order of the text

The text begins at verse 1 when the disciples ask, "Who is the greatest in the kingdom of heaven?" Out of this question comes a story calling the disciples to understand the kingdom in a new way.

> [23]"Therefore, the kingdom of heaven is like a king who wanted to settle accounts with his servants. [24]As he began the settlement, a man who owed him ten thousand talents was brought to him. [25]Since he was not able to pay, the master ordered that he and his wife and his children and all that he had be sold to repay the debt."

"Therefore" (*dia touto*) means "on account of this," referring to Peter's conversation with the Lord:

> [21]Then Peter came to Jesus and asked, "Lord, how many times shall I forgive my brother when he sins against me? Up to seven times?"
> [22]Jesus answered, "I tell you, not seven times, but seventy-seven times."

Matthew links up the coming story with Jesus' seventy-seven times statement, that there is no limit to the number of times we are to forgive.

Jesus' opening line tells of a king who rules his domain as one would expect, by the rules. The listener assumes that, like a banker, he will collect what is owed to him. The issue is not about what the tax collector did or the servant's relationship to his master. It is simply about the king getting back what is owed him. There is no reason to expect the king to do otherwise; it makes perfect sense for the one owed money to insist on repayment.

The servant, by his position, has power. He is bright, tough, strategic, and deliberate, doing nothing out of feelings or kindness, as such people do not survive in such places of power. Over the years, this man has built relationships with clients. He is powerful; the sum he owes tells us that.

> [26]"The servant fell on his knees before him. 'Be patient with me,' he begged, 'and I will pay back everything.'"

The servant, in asking the king to "be bighearted," begs for time to repay.

Reeling from the astronomical amount he has to pay, those listening would have broken into laughter at his outlandish promise, "I'll repay it all." How incredible! There is no possibility that the servant could repay it. It is here the hearer realizes that Jesus has set up an impossible scenario—the $9 billion owed and a promise to repay it—to make a point.

> [27]"The servant's master took pity on him, canceled the debt and let him go."

The servant is slick. He assumes the king is just another "bookkeeper" (Capon 1988, 47), interested only in money. And to add to the seeming naïveté of the king, he seems to fall for the servant's promise to repay. The king, defying expectations, cancels the debt and, by so doing, takes on the burden of debt by depleting his wealth to remove the certain poverty and suffering of his servant.

> [28]"But when that servant went out, he found one of his fellow servants who owed him a hundred denarii. He grabbed him and began to choke him. 'Pay back what you owe me!' he demanded.
> [29]"His fellow servant fell to his knees and begged him, 'Be patient with me, and I will pay you back.' [30]"But he refused.

> Instead, he went off and had the man thrown into prison until he could pay the debt."

With the heat off, the servant, oblivious to the nature of his own forgiveness, stumbles into self-centered actions by coming down hard on another who owes him much less.

How tragic and stupid is the servant! Having just been forgiven billions of dollars, he grabs one of his debtors (a *syndoulos*—a fellow slave, probably on a lower bureaucratic level than himself) by the scruff of the neck and hauls him off to debtor's prison (McBride, 116).

The parable is so far-fetched that the audience would have found it difficult not to smile at this cartoon figure (Capon 1988, 48)— that is, until they saw in him the greed most understood too well in themselves. How soon the servant forgot the enormous debt the king absorbed! It is as if the servant believed he was worthy of forgiveness as he blundered into a reversal of his good fortune. The servant instead acts like the bookkeeper he expected the king to be. Failing to see the nature of the king and failing to follow in his steps, he yields to his own greed.

There is a schizophrenic pattern of behavior in the parable. For a good part of his life the servant has lived within the pattern of his master's world. But just after being released from an enormous debt, he flips and aggressively seeks out one who owes him. He ends up not so much tragic as stupid. Or could it be that since he had known only ruthless behavior all his life—before the king did any negotiation, he ordered the servant's wife and children to be sold— now that he is freed he still knows nothing other than ruthlessness? In other words, the gift of freedom was so unconventional and new that to him it meant nothing. He was unable to absorb the meaning of being forgiven, at least sufficiently to modify how he acted toward one of his fellow servants. Forgiveness did not transform him. The very skills that had made him an effective servant to the king, extracting tax and tribute, now lead to his downfall.

The manager, coming out of the king's residence, appears to want to consolidate his position and reassert his control. No sooner has he wondered how he could rebuild his tattered reputation than along comes a middle-level bureaucrat who owes him money. To show his power to a skeptical bureaucracy, he takes the poor fellow by the throat and demands immediate repayment. The amount was not small—about a Roman legionnaire's annual salary—but in comparison to what the manager had owed it was nothing.

> [31]"When the other servants saw what had happened, they were greatly distressed and went and told their master everything that had happened.

Others in the community of managers were outraged, as they had every right to be. There existed then what Herzog calls "retainers" (Herzog, 144), those who provided funding within the bizarre world of exploiting rulers and bureaucrats who managed the flow of money and debt. For this servant to turn on another would upset the balance within the system. The rumors of the servant's reaction would ripple their way through the ruling groups. Not surprisingly, they told the king.

> [32]"Then the master called the servant in. 'You wicked servant,' he said, 'I canceled all that debt of yours because you begged me to. [33]Shouldn't you have had mercy on your fellow servant just as I had on you?' [34]In anger his master turned him over to the jailers to be tortured, until he should pay back all he owed."

In choosing to ignore the nature of life offered by forgiveness, the servant chose the life of death. For it was not the master who brought the servant into death, it was his own actions that pushed him from freedom into misery and death.

We are not told why the king forgave. As well, the question as to why the king allowed that amount of debt to build up before being detected is left out.

> [35]"This is how my heavenly Father will treat each of you unless you forgive your brother from your heart."

Hultgren views this verse as "hortatory by intent, not a dogmatic statement for all time" (Hultgren, 29), meaning that this verse is not to be interpreted that God forgives us only as we forgive or that our forgiveness is a precondition for his forgiveness. Rather, as Capon notes, it is not our debts that keep us from grace; it is our refusal to live in grace and forgiveness:

> If we refuse to die—and in particular, if we insist on bind-
> ing others' debts upon them in the name of our own right to
> life—we will, by not letting grace have its way *through* us, cut
> ourselves off from ever knowing the joy of grace *in us.* (Capon
> 1988, 50)

David Buttrick assumes this verse was an add-on (Buttrick, 108,
112–13; also note Hultgren, 30). Because Jesus seems to say that
God's forgiveness is based on our works, Buttrick discounts them
as being Jesus' words.

Capon's approach, however, seems more useful: "I propose to
take his words as ironic" (Capon 1988, 43). Within the story there is
a sense of covenant, in that one's relationship with God is not one-
way. God's forgiveness invites a covenant response. Life comes from
understanding forgiveness, which in turn leads to acts of forgiveness, without which the nature of God's gift cannot be understood.
Jesus says, in effect, "So is everyone who doesn't forgive his brother
from *his heart.*" The reason the servant did not forgive is that nothing had happened in his heart when he was forgiven.

Homiletical considerations

1. The challenge in preaching this parable to postmoderns is to
move toward personal transformation. The final words of Jesus in
this text are key: "So is everyone who doesn't forgive his brother
from *his heart.*" Forgiveness is more than ethical behavior, for
being able to meet those standards implies the correctly set inner
compass that points the person in the right direction. What is
needed, then, is the inner change of the *heart* so that the person
is able to live differently. The end of the sermon should bring the
hearer to understand the need to be transformed. As good as the
lessons of this parable are and the variety of secular places it would
find a hearing, this is not just about good behavior: It is about the
personal change from which springs an intuitive response to be
good.

2. Jesus is a master at the use of hyperbole: a debt of $9 billion!
This alerts the hearer.

3. Because the parable takes up the entire pericope, the preacher
could allow the parable to be the framework for the message.

4. The major movements within this parable are:

a.   There is a time when all of God's people will be called to account: their sins—$9 billion worth—will be forgiven by God's gift of grace.
b.   Stunted minds and hearts forget what has been forgiven; the greedy side of life is in control, and the end is worse than the beginning.
c.   Jesus reminds this people that how they handle his forgiveness will have an impact on how he deals with them.

Parable Three:
Laborers in the Vineyard (Matthew 20:1-16)

Text

[1]"For the kingdom of heaven is like a landowner who went out early in the morning to hire men to work in his vineyard. [2]He agreed to pay them a denarius for the day and sent them into his vineyard.

[3]"About the third hour he went out and saw others standing in the marketplace doing nothing. [4]He told them, 'You also go and work in my vineyard, and I will pay you whatever is right.' [5]So they went.

"He went out again about the sixth hour and the ninth hour and did the same thing. [6]About the eleventh hour he went out and found still others standing around. He asked them, 'Why have you been standing here all day long doing nothing?'

[7]"'Because no one has hired us,' they answered.

"He said to them, 'You also go and work in my vineyard.'

[8]"When evening came, the owner of the vineyard said to his foreman, 'Call the workers and pay them their wages, beginning with the last ones hired and going on to the first.'

[9]"The workers who were hired about the eleventh hour came and each received a denarius. [10]So when those came who were hired first, they expected to receive more. But each one of them also received a denarius. [11]When they received it, they began to grumble against the landowner. [12]'These men who were hired last worked only one hour,' they said, 'and you have made them equal to us who have borne the burden of the work and the heat of the day.'

[13]"But he answered one of them, 'Friend, I am not being unfair to you. Didn't you agree to work for a denarius? [14]Take your pay

and go. I want to give the man who was hired last the same as I gave you. [15]Don't I have the right to do what I want with my own money? Or are you envious because I am generous?'

[16]"So the last will be first, and the first will be last."

This parable's unique preaching window to postmoderns

Postmodern culture has been in part defined by democracy and its offspring, human rights. As postmoderns listen and read this parable, labor/management issues of fairness and equity become most evident.

The business model of power—as developed in the age of modernity—is rejected by an egalitarian postmodernism. While the language of power and authority of business and labor often obviate market-driven reality, the instinctive response to this parable is, "Where is fairness?" Fairness and equity are the windows that open the listener to hear Jesus' concerns.

Position of the parable within the text

Jesus' parables fit within three time periods of ministry: (1) those told in Galilee, focusing on the kingdom; (2) those told while in Perea, dealing with relationships of the person and the kingdom; and (3) those told during passion week, speaking about judgment. This parable belongs in the third category, just as the crucifixion casts a long shadow across Jesus' life (Hanko, 242).

Even though Matthew places this parable during the passion week, Jesus may have given this parable at other times. It should not be assumed that this would have been the only time that the grumbling Pharisees had heard Jesus tell it.

It follows three important sections in Matthew: (1) Jesus' conversation with the Pharisees on divorce and their misreading of the law (19:1-12); (2) Jesus' rebuke of his disciples in which he illustrates those of the kingdom—children, the most inexperienced of people—(19:13-15); and (3) a conversation with a rich young man whom he tells to sell everything and follow him (19:16-26). In each of these, Jesus reverses conventional wisdom.

It all begins with Peter's concern, given they have left all to follow Jesus, will there be any reward for them in the end (19:27-30)? Jesus reassures them that "at the renewal of all things" they will sit on twelve thrones. He assures them of his care: "and everyone who has left houses or brothers or sisters or father or mother or children or fields for my sake will receive a hundred times as much and will inherit eternal life" (v. 29). However, to clarify that their reward is not based on their getting what they think they should, Jesus says, "But many who are first will be last, and many who are last will be first" (v. 30) and follows with this parable. He closes, "So the last will be first, and the first will be last" (20:16).

Word study

Landowner or "Lord"—oikodespotes. The "lord" is head of the house (20:1, 3, 5), which makes it strange that a person of such prestige and wealth would be personally recruiting workers.

Agora. The marketplace where the master went to find recruits.

Denarius. Usually seen as an average day's wage for a laborer (Scott 1989, 290–91).

The Foreman—kyrios. The foreman is not the owner who did the hiring or firing of the workforce but a member of management (Hultgren, 33).

Friend—hetaior. This kind of friend does not imply friendliness. If the landowner were addressing a social equal he would have used *phile* (Herzog, 92).

Cultural factors

The Setting. What these men were paid—a denarius—was not a great deal of money, but equal to what a family would need for a day.

The story begins with the landowner hiring workers, probably at harvesttime when the farmer would have only a few days to harvest the grapes. An experienced farmer knows that one day can make an enormous difference in realizing the potential of the harvest. So it is not surprising for the owner to return throughout the day to find more workers. In monitoring the amount taken by the workers, if the daily quota was low, he would increase the number of workers.

In first-century Palestinian culture, the day laborer was on the lowest rung of the economic ladder (Young, 70), on the margins of survival, finding work wherever possible. Such pools of day laborers were populated by peasant sons who had not received land from their parents and therefore had no means to support their families. They would have to compete with others for daily work on large estates (Herzog, 90).

Gathering grapes was tough manual labor. The "heat of the day" is no cliché. The heat of high noon in the Middle East is notorious, a reminder to those listening how hard a job it was.

This parable is not an implicit instruction by Jesus on management theory. Jesus gives no indication that he was promoting a certain economic or labor theory or practice (Herzog, 84–89). This is a story only about his kingdom.

The obvious tension here is between our natural empathy with the full-day workers' sense of being treated unfairly and the belief that the owner (who symbolizes God) would never be unfair. The question running just beneath the surface is, What about fairness? Within today's labor laws—founded on the notion of equity and equal treatment for all—for this landowner to give those who worked less the same as those who worked longer violates assumptions of fair labor/management practices.

Subject
How does God reward us?

Complement
God rewards us with generosity and not according to our accomplishments.

The surprise
It is not surprising that those who worked the full day received pay according to their agreement, but it is surprising that those who worked less than a full day were paid the same wage. This, however, is not learned until the end of the parable. The owner begins by handing out one denarius to the ones who had worked only one hour. This raised expectations among those who worked the entire day: Their reasoning was, if those who worked only one hour got one denarius, then those of us who worked a full day will surely get more than that.

The workers who began early in the morning—as they watched those who worked much less of the day get a full day's wage—thought they were dealing with a generous owner. Imagine their shock when they received exactly what they had agreed on, which was the same amount as those who had worked only one hour.

Exegetical outline

I. An owner of a vineyard recruits laborers to work in his fields (vv. 1-7).
    A. Laborers are recruited throughout the day.
        i.   Recruitment begins in the early morning.
        ii. The second wave of recruitment is at 9:00 A.M.
        iii. The landowner continues to recruit at noon and 3:00 P.M.
        iv. Finally, he picks up more workers at 5:00 P.M.
    B. The owner decides on his payment for work done.
        i.   The early laborers agreed on one denarius for the day.
        ii. The others are not given any promise except that the pay will be fair.
II. The steward pays the workers in the evening (vv. 8-15).
    A. Payment is made first to those recruited last.
        i.   Those who worked only one hour get the same as promised to those who worked a full day.
        ii. There is expectation among those recruited first that they will get more than the amount to which they agreed.
        iii. To their dismay, everyone gets exactly the same.
    B. Those hired first complain this is unfair.
        i.   They have worked all day.
        ii. They have also worked during the hottest time of the day.
    C. The owner makes his rebuttal.
        i.   I paid you what had been agreed.
        ii. It is my desire to be generous to the last workers.
        iii. Is the real problem that you are envious of the others?
III. Jesus provides a homiletical wrap-up to the parable (v. 16).
    A. He ends as he began, with the principle of his kingdom— the last being first and the first being last.

Homiletical outline

I. It is God who calls us from unproductive activity to God's kingdom work.
   A. It is not surprising that the condition of being employed by the Father is based first on God's call and then on our willingness.
      i. God chooses all kinds of people to work in God's kingdom.
      ii. God also chooses people out of all sorts of circumstances.
   B. The compensation is God's choice.
      i. We all expect fairness in our reward.
      ii. Not unlike the disciples, we are anxious that we will be treated fairly.
II. It is God who, in the end, determines our compensation.
   A. We are inclined to believe that reward is connected directly to our productivity.
      i. We slip into the notion that our reward is a direct result of our work.
      ii. We compare our reward to that of others, believing ours should be greater.
   B. We learn that God's kingdom works differently than does the kingdom of evil.

The big idea

God's kingdom works differently than does the kingdom of the world.

The challenge here, as in all parables, is to discover the vision of God. Jesus points out the unmerited generosity by which God calls and welcomes the outcast into the community of faith. All are made equal.

It is almost as if Jesus is teasing Peter and the disciples, trying to help them understand the generous nature of God. Concerned that a rich man cannot enter the kingdom, the disciples wonder on what kind of rewards could they count, to which Jesus reminds them to rest in God's fairness and generosity.

Material in order of the text

1"For the kingdom of heaven is like a landowner who went out early in the morning to hire men to work in his vineyard."

Vineyards were owned by the elite, not the average farmer. Their product—wine—could be converted into a luxury item and exported, providing a good return on the investment. It required, however, at least four years of investment in the planting and pruning of the vines before any profit might be realized. This suggests that the owner had the capital required for such a long-term investment, implying that he was a man of wealth (Herzog, 84–85).

This scene is familiar in many countries, where men sit by the side of the road early in the morning, waiting for people from farms and factories to drive by in trucks, picking up available workers. These people are not slaves, but rather workers with no permanent jobs, people without any sort of economic or social security.

While the landowner fits as a metaphor for God, some scholars view the landowner "as a member of an oppressing elite class" (Herzog, 96). If, however, we assume that the parable is about the action of an oppressive elite and not a window into the heart of God, we ignore the setting of the parable. Rather than trying to see it through twenty-first-century experience, in preaching this parable it is more consistent with biblical scholarship to look for the central theme and search out Jesus' purpose in telling it.

> [2]"He agreed to pay them a denarius for the day and sent them into his vineyard."

A denarius was an average day's pay for a laborer. Although there is debate over the actual level of income this provided (Scott 1989, 291), Herzog assumes this was a fair wage (Herzog, 89–90).

We are reminded that the owner goes out to recruit a number of times in the day, negotiating with the earliest group and then simply telling the others that he will give them what is fair. The reason for including the owner's activity in the narrative seems to be more added color than a homiletical directive.

> [3]"About the third hour he went out and saw others standing in the marketplace doing nothing."

The third hour is 9:00 A.M.

The listener might wonder why the owner did not know in the morning how many workers he needed, instead of going out three more times during the day. As with most of his parables, Jesus constructs this to suit his purposes. There is no need to make all the elements fit together as in an actual event. The frequent hiring serves the story by developing a pattern, so that when payment is made at the end of the day the hearer is pushed to ask the question the workers hired earlier in the day ask.

> [4]"He told them, 'You also go and work in my vineyard, and I will pay you whatever is right.' [5]So they went."

At this point the hearer is introduced to the question that will need to be answered: How much will the workers receive? This gives the story direction.

> [5]"He went out again about the sixth hour and the ninth hour and did the same thing."

The sixth hour is noon and the ninth hour is 3:00 P.M.

These two excursions serve to reinforce what has just gone on: More workers have been hired without any agreement as to payment, which forces the question, What will they get?

> [6]"About the eleventh hour he went out and found still others standing around. He asked them, 'Why have you been standing here all day long doing nothing?'"

The eleventh hour is 5:00 P.M.

The question can be read either as humor—people listening would chuckle—or as a caustic critique of their self-imposed situation—"the reason you guys aren't working is because you are lazy!" However, the word for "standing around" means "without work." There is no sense that they were unemployed because they were lazy (Hultgren, 38).

But why does the landowner need more laborers? Or does he? What difference will workers putting in only one hour make? While these are interesting questions, they are not germane to the parable.

> [7]"'Because no one has hired us,' they answered.
> "He said to them, 'You also go and work in my vineyard.'"

If the parable had ended here it would link up with Jesus' call to work in his harvest: "The harvest is plentiful but the workers are few. Ask the Lord of the harvest, therefore, to send out workers into his harvest field" (Matt. 9:37-38). This is not his intent, however.

This parable points out an important element in Jesus' parables: While there is significant story time devoted to the workers, there is no hint as to their personality or character. Jesus doesn't provide psychological or emotional insight; instead, he simply tells the story. *What* the owner does is key to an understanding of Jesus' response to Peter's question (19:27).

> [8]"When evening came, the owner of the vineyard said to his foreman, 'Call the workers and pay them their wages, beginning with the last ones hired and going on to the first.'"

The hearer expects now to learn the answer to the question, What is right? One's vision of God grows as the one-hour workers get a full day's pay: "What incredible generosity!" Peter might have thought. While the listener now believes that those who worked longer will get even more than what they had agreed, Jesus takes the story in another direction.

> [9]"The workers who were hired about the eleventh hour came and each received a denarius. [10]So when those came who were hired first, they expected to receive more. But each one of them also received a denarius."

The sequence of paying sets the listener up for a surprise. Expectations rise among those who worked all day: "If these guys who only worked one hour get the same amount I agreed to for the whole day, just imagine what I'll get for working twelve hours."

The listener assumes that their expectations are fair. But as the story unfolds, listeners share in the sense of injustice. The tension measurably increases because the owner is a metaphor for God. There is an uneasiness: On one hand, the listener wants to believe that God is just, and yet, on the other hand, feels the seeming injustice that underwrites the complaints of the workers who have been there the entire day.

> [11]"When they received it, they began to grumble against the landowner. [12]'These men who were hired last worked only one hour,' they said, 'and you have made them equal to us who have borne the burden of the work and the heat of the day.'"

Those who worked the entire day are who charge the landowner with injustice: first, that he fails to take into account that they worked longer; and second, that they worked during the hottest time of the day. In the end—so they reason—because they all got the same they were unfairly treated (Hultgren, 38).

Herzog suggests another interpretation (Herzog, 91–93): The order of payment is an insult as the listener senses there is something unfair about it all. Could it be that they were being told that their long workday, through the heat of the day, had not been valued any more than the work of those who worked just one hour? Was this—as Herzog sees it—a way of keeping the oppressed under control? For if the laborers revolt this late in the day, they do it to their disadvantage because of the sheer numbers of laborers available. The next day, when the owner comes to recruit, he can easily pass them by and find others. So they are shamed into submission. They have no option. "He threatens their status as expendables. They must respond" (Herzog, 92).

Another interpretation is that the twelve-hour workers "are defining their personal worth in contrast to others; they are not so much angered by what happened to them as envious of the good fortune of the other workers. They are so enclosed in their understanding of justice that it becomes a norm by which they become judges of others. They want to order the world by their norms, which limit the master's freedom and exclude unexpected generosity. . . . What began as an act of goodness to them and unfolded as an act of generosity to others blinded them to the goodness of the owner and the good fortune of others" (Donahue 1988, 82).

> [13]"But he answered one of them, 'Friend, I am not being unfair to you. Didn't you agree to work for a denarius?'"

The Greek word for "friend"—*hetaior*—is not a statement of friendliness; it is the same word Jesus used when he confronted Judas in Gethsemane. "It is condescending and subtly reinforces their different social stations, yet it feigns courtesy. If he were addressing a social equal he would have used *phile*" (Herzog, 92).

At this point, the owner tries to reason with the workers. There is even a sense that he wants to know from them if he has done something wrong.

> [14]"Take your pay and go. I want to give the man who was hired last the same as I gave you. [15]Don't I have the right to do what I want with my own money? Or are you envious because I am generous?"

The literal translation of "Or are you envious because I am generous?" is "Or is your eye evil because I am good?" (Hultgren, 39), suggesting that the eye of the person grumbling is one of envy, greedy for what is beyond his proper share.

Brad Young provides this translation: "Am I not permitted to do with mine as I want? Even if your eye is evil, mine is [I am] good?" The idiom *evil eye* is an "accusation of a stinginess [which] was an insult that carried with it a certain measure of shame. Generosity was a virtue that was highly esteemed in Jewish culture" (Young, 79). Jesus contrasts the landowner's generosity with the workers who ignore the good fortune of the others.

Jesus' words suggest a "what is mine is thine" Jewish saying:

> What is mine is mine and what is thine is thine—this person is average.
>   What is mine is thine and what is thine is mine—this person is ignorant.
>   What is thine is mine and what is mine is mine—this person is wicked.
>   What is mine is thine and what is thine is thine—this person is a saint. (Young, 79–80)

The landowner makes two rebuttals: First, they got what they had agreed on, so no injustice was committed; and second, his generosity to some does not imply injustice to others (Hultgren, 39).

Breech notes four components to their grumbling:

a. Those who grumble do so because of envy—their "evil eye."
b. Their sense of dignity is challenged.
c. A means by which their self-worth is established is challenged in that they end up comparing themselves to others.
d. While they envy the good fortune of those who worked only a few hours, they end up blaming the landowner. (Breech 1983, 150)

Those who began work in the early part of the day were not pleased that those who started later in the day received generous pay. Why were they not willing to celebrate the good fortune of their coworkers (Young, 78)? Did not they see how this generosity would ripple down into the well-being of their families? Instead, envious of what their coworkers got, they end up grumbling that they got less than they thought was fair.

> [16]"So the last will be first, and the first will be last."

Here Jesus presses home a principle of his kingdom: Regardless of when a person joins or the amount of work done, each is loved and regarded as essential. The Pharisees, who fussed about the keeping of many laws, are also regarded as having value, but they are to understand that those who do not rate on their level of performance may go to the front of the line. "Jesus does not condemn the Pharisees but warns that a desire to live justly according to the covenant should not lead to an attitude that dictates to the covenant God how mercy and generosity should be shown. The line between following God's will and *deciding what God wills* is always thin and fragile" (Donahue 1988, 83).

Homiletical considerations

The challenge of preaching this parable to postmoderns is to move them past their concern over equity to the consideration of the source of life itself. This parable pushes the hearer to trust in God above what we might consider to be fair.

1. Preaching this parable requires that in answering Peter's question—"So what will we get?"—the congregation is led into a confession of faith. This confession can help the postmodern to make the source of fairness the center of faith and not fairness itself—the point being that God, who by faith they have come to trust, will indeed reward them on God's ruling of fairness and equity and not theirs. For some, this is a leap, but one this parable enables.

2. These issues—fairness and personal compensation—need to be highlighted so as to make sure the hearers know what is at stake in the story. Without making this clear, the parable will lose its unique appeal and Jesus' message will not be learned in the application.

3. In preaching this text, stay away from making it into a prescription for management. It is atypical of how one expects organizations to work, and because of that its surprise makes the parable memorable.

4. It serves the lessons of the parable if the preacher plays on the natural tension within the story. Jesus surprises the listeners: Just when they think they know the outcome, he reverses their expectations and they end up learning a kingdom principle. He assured the disciples that they are special and in the end they will be well rewarded. But he also wants them to know that some they assume will not be rewarded—here or in eternity—will be.

5. It seems that the more religious some people become, the greater is their tendency to confine God's justice within a strict religious formula in which reward is equal to merit. God's mercy challenges the disciples to move beyond their own narrow sense of justice to understand that "God's ways are not our ways."

6. There are three major movements that the listeners need to hear:

a.   The opening part of the sermon needs to set up Peter's question, a question we all seem to ask at some time: "What then will there be for us?"

b.   This leads to the next movement, in which God calls the listener to do God's work.

c.   The great reversal is the surprise for those who worked all day and those who started at 5:00 P.M.

Parable Four: Talents (Matthew 25:14-30)

Text

[14]"Again, it will be like a man going on a journey, who called his servants and entrusted his property to them. [15]To one he gave five talents of money, to another two talents, and to another one talent, each according to his ability. Then he went on his journey. [16]The man who had received the five talents went at once and put his money to work and gained five more. [17]So also, the one with the two talents gained two more. [18]But the man who had received the one talent went off, dug a hole in the ground and hid his master's money.

[19]"After a long time the master of those servants returned and settled accounts with them. [20]The man who had received the five talents brought the other five. 'Master,' he said, 'you entrusted me with five talents. See, I have gained five more.'

[21]"His master replied, 'Well done, good and faithful servant! You have been faithful with a few things; I will put you in charge of many things. Come and share your master's happiness!'

²²"The man with the two talents also came. 'Master,' he said, 'you entrusted me with two talents; see, I have gained two more.'

²³"His master replied, 'Well done, good and faithful servant! You have been faithful with a few things; I will put you in charge of many things. Come and share your master's happiness!'

²⁴"Then the man who had received the one talent came. 'Master,' he said, 'I knew that you are a hard man, harvesting where you have not sown and gathering where you have not scattered seed. ²⁵So I was afraid and went out and hid your talent in the ground. See, here is what belongs to you.'

²⁶"His master replied, 'You wicked, lazy servant! So you knew that I harvest where I have not sown and gather where I have not scattered seed? ²⁷Well then, you should have put my money on deposit with the bankers, so that when I returned I would have received it back with interest.

²⁸"'Take the talent from him and give it to the one who has the ten talents. ²⁹For everyone who has will be given more, and he will have an abundance. Whoever does not have, even what he has will be taken from him. ³⁰And throw that worthless servant outside, into the darkness, where there will be weeping and gnashing of teeth.'"

This parable's unique preaching window to postmoderns

Increasing numbers of people are investing in stock markets, whether through pensions funds or directly. With one's future economic well-being increasingly dependent on the profitability of a stock or fund, more North Americans better understand the relationship between investing and profitability. Tracking one's investment has gone beyond being the pastime activities of the rich; it is essential for the middle class's security in retirement. This parable, built on making profit by good investment, will attract the postmodern. Added to that is the matter of fairness and equity. It seems, at first reading, that what the third servant experiences is outrageous. These two elements—investment and fairness—unite in creating a compelling story for postmoderns.

Position of the parable within the text

From Matt. 24:3 onward, Jesus speaks to his disciples about the following: the signs of the end of the age; the importance of being ready; the importance of managing his investments. These messages raise awareness with his disciples that soon Jesus will leave.

The implied question is, How are his followers to work during his absence?

Word study

Talent. From the Greek *talanton*, this refers to an actual measurement of wealth. The master in this parable uses cash, a means of trade increasingly common in first-century Palestine.

One talent was worth 6,000 denarii (Hultgren, 274–75) and one denarius about a day's labor, thus making the talent worth about twenty years' wages. (Compared to a salary today of $40,000, five talents or 30,000 denarii would amount to approximately $1,800,000.)

Cultural factors

Social Structure. First-century Palestinian social structure was in part based on the elite who provided the basis for economic life and oversaw its political life (Herzog, 156).

Owners of estates relied on their household bureaucracy to run the enterprise. The owners would often travel, building connections and making deals to further their enterprises, during which times they trusted their senior management to ensure ongoing success.

Subject

How can we please the Lord as we await his return?

Complement

We please the Lord by taking risks with what God has given us.

The surprise

Listeners are surprised to hear Jesus say that in his kingdom, failure to risk is sin. In other parables, sin is seen as drunkenness or beating one's servants. Here, the one charged with being "wicked" has done none of the above, but is a rather prudent servant, anxious not to lose the original asset.

Jesus takes his listeners by surprise as the third servant, by exercising caution, gets the opposite of the first two. "Precaution is usually esteemed as a virtue, but it often becomes excessive, preventing creativity and stifling productivity. The precaution of the one-talent servant caused a financial reversal and resulted in his punishment" (Young, 92).

Though he attempted to justify his inaction by his knowledge of the master, the servant had let fear keep him from the possibility of failure by burying the money. In trying to preserve the capital, he lost what he could have gained.

Exegetical outline

I. Before the owner of an estate takes a journey, he speaks to three of his trusted servants (vv. 14-15).
    A. He gives them money to invest.
    B. The obvious expectation is that they will make a return on the capital he has placed in their keeping.

II. The owner returns from his journey and compliments the two servants on investing well (vv. 19-23).
    A. The first man is congratulated on doubling the investment.
    B. The second man is also congratulated on doubling the investment.

III. The third man gives an explanation as to why he has nothing to show for a return (vv. 24-25).
    A. He was afraid of his master.
    B. In his fear he buried the money rather than invest it.

IV. The owner responds to the servant who buried the money (vv. 26-30).
    A. He admits that he reaps where he has not sown.
    B. He asks why the servant did not at least invest the money with the bank.
    C. He takes what he had given to the third servant and gives it to the first one.
    D. He throws the third servant out of his employ.

Homiletical outline

I. Like Jesus' disciples we await his return.
    A. While we wait we are given "gifts," which Jesus expects us to invest.
    B. We are invested with his power, helping us do what Christ expects of us.

II. Christ will return and review what we have done with our "gifts."
   A. Those who have served by risking will be praised.
   B. Excuses of being afraid will not pass his test.
III. There is an awful consequence for those who "bury" the opportunities of faith.
   A. The great sin is that of unfaith.
   B. We ultimately gain by risking in opportunities.

The big idea

Use it or lose it.

God's followers are expected to so trust God that they will risk in opportunities. Called to live by faith, they are not to fear. It is fear that leads to sin, while faith leads to pleasing God. Jesus points out that it is better to risk what one has and lose it than to risk nothing and retain the initial investment.

Material in order of the text

> [14]"Again it will be like a man going on a journey, who called his servants and entrusted his property to them."

Jesus sets up a plausible story of a master/servant relationship. Of course, it is only the wealthy who could leave home and go to a far country, having servants who would look after the home place and the master's assets. There is, however, no sense that the master is testing his servants. This is too much money for the master to use as a test (Herzog, 158).

> [15]"To one he gave five talents of money, to another two talents, and to another one talent, each according to his ability. Then he went on his journey."

The master gives no direction as to how they were to invest the capital. Out of their respective experiences and places of power they were to go about making their investments.

The assignment was an opportunity to increase the value of the household. Though each was different, each was given opportunity. The text "each according to his ability" may be better read as "each according to his power or social position." The master, who understood each servant, gave them an opportunity he believed they could manage within the time he was away (Herzog, 158).

> [16]"The man who had received the five talents went at once and put his money to work and gained five more."

The phrase "went at once and put his money to work" suggests that "he worked with the talents at his disposal, and in this case it will mean specifically that he engaged in business, although the listener is not told what kind" (Hultgren, 275).

It was customary for those charged with increasing the master's assets to take a slice for themselves. In improving his net worth, they could realize personal gain from the increase (Herzog, 160).

> [17]"So also, the one with the two talents gained two more."

The second servant, with no hesitation, moved immediately to make the money work.

> [18]"But the man who had received the one talent went off, dug a hole in the ground and hid his master's money."

As much as he wanted to please his master, this servant gave up any future potential by taking the least risky approach possible. By burying the money he gave up on increasing the capital. By so doing, he misunderstood the master's character, even though he later says he understood him. "His good intention, misled by a wrong understanding of his master, produced the opposite result. . . . According to the message of the parable, good intentions are not enough" (Young, 83).

> [19]"After a long time the master of those servants returned and settled accounts with them."

The word for "master"—kurios—is "Lord," suggesting that Jesus speaks of himself.

As well, the leaving and returning of the master implies Jesus is speaking of himself and that the coming parousia was the coming of the king.

> [20]"The man who had received the five talents brought the other five. 'Master,' he said, 'you entrusted me with five talents. See, I have gained five more.'"

The servant returns 100 percent increase for the master.

> [21]"His master replied, 'Well done, good and faithful servant! You have been faithful with a few things; I will put you in charge of many things. Come and share your master's happiness!'
> [22]"The man with the two talents also came. 'Master,' he said, 'you entrusted me with two talents; see, I have gained two more.'
> [23]"His master replied, 'Well done, good and faithful servant! You have been faithful with a few things; I will put you in charge of many things. Come and share your master's happiness!'"

Their gain indicates successful use of the funds in investment, no small feat. The amount gained, however, is not what is of final importance to the owner, but rather that the workers invested with a view to an increase.

On the basis of their success they are given added responsibilities, and while the master calls their amounts "little," they really are large amounts and represent an enormous trust by the master.

> [24]"Then the man who had received the one talent came. 'Master,' he said, 'I knew that you are a hard man, harvesting where you have not sown and gathering where you have not scattered seed. [25]So I was afraid and went out and hid your talent in the ground. See, here is what belongs to you.'"

Here is the climax of the story: What now will the master do with the third servant?

Note the irony in the imagery: He knows his master reaps where he has not sown, yet he buries the money, which means there is no increase. In calling him a "hard" man, he attributes to his master what is not seen; in fact, the master seems quite magnanimous, entrusting so much to his servants.

> [26]"His master replied, 'You wicked, lazy servant! So you knew that I harvested where I have not sown and gather where I have not scattered seed?"

Though he is called "wicked," that is not meant in a moral sense but is because he failed to abide by the opportunity and instructions of his master.

The master responds to the third servant by taking what he had and gives it to the first. What seems to be at work here—and is reinforced by verse 29—is that those who take advantage of opportunities become more able to respond to future opportunities.

> [27]"'Well then, you should have put my money on deposit with the bankers, so that when I returned I would have received it back with interest.'"

If the servant did not have the fortitude to risk in an investment, the master reasons, the least he could have done was to place it with moneylenders. The servant's concern, however, was his own well-being. Rather than being faithful and taking risks for the benefit and well-being of his master, he hid the money.

> [28]"'Take the talent from him and give it to the one who has the ten talents.
>
> [29]'For everyone who has will be given more, and he will have an abundance. Whoever does not have, even what he has will be taken from him.
>
> [30]'And throw that worthless servant outside, into the darkness, where there will be weeping and gnashing of teeth.'"

The master's judgment seems unfair. Arland Hultgren sees it this way: "[W]herever God's gift has already borne fruit, God gives in greater abundance; where it has been fruitless, it is lost completely" (Hultgren, 277).

The third servant is judged because he acted not out of faith but out of prudence. He operated on the basis of what he thought he knew about the master rather than following his instructions.

Homiletical considerations

1. The challenge in telling this story to a postmodern is to move beyond its being a story of entrepreneurial success or failure to point out that each person is accountable to God. While accountability is set within the call to risk investing, the issue is not what gifts God

has given but that God expects people to risk. In the end, people will be judged on their willingness to do just that.

2. The parable was told to the disciples and not the Pharisees. Risk taking was not a message designed for the bookkeeping Pharisees; instead, Jesus spoke to his followers. His warning is rather straightforward: There should be no doubt as to what he expects upon his return.

3. While in this parable "talents" is about real money and not the same usage of "talents" today, yet Peter's words—"Each one should use whatever gift he has received to serve others, faithfully administering God's grace in its various forms"—comes into play (1 Peter 4:10). Everyone is given gifts (Rom. 12:6; 1 Cor. 12:4ff.) and "talents" are symbolic of what God entrusts to us.

4. The challenge this parable brings to the pulpit is the need to refute the assumption that being cautious is better than risking; preserving is better than taking a chance at improvement; holding is better than giving; a consistently good balance sheet is better than a measured risk for growth. This parable disabuses the view that God will not judge what people do with their gifts and opportunities. What it does is to put out in front unashamedly the notion of accountability. Grace notwithstanding, all will be examined on the basis of industriousness. Preach with care, but do not avoid its implications!

5. As with other parables, there should not be imposed on the story any contemporary economic model, be it free-enterprise capitalism or democratic socialism.

6. People will resonate with the nature of this parable. Increasingly more people manage their own pension portfolios and are aware of what it means to risk in investment so as to gain a reasonable return. This story, based on finance and investment risk, will be of great interest.

7. Some will question which side the poor who heard this story were on. Would they have sided with the third servant or sympathized with his predicament? Because this story is given to the disciples, such questions are not germane to its understanding, nor are they helpful in drawing out homiletical lessons.

8. The minefield is to make this into a guilt trip. The issue is not what happens to those who fail to meet up with the master's expectations—note that the only expectation is in taking a risk and making

the investment—but rather the opportunities he provides. In essence, it is a story that shows how much people's lives matter to God.

Parable Five:
The Good Samaritan (Luke 10:25-37)

Text

[25]On one occasion an expert in the law stood up to test Jesus. "Teacher," he asked, "what must I do to inherit eternal life?"

[26]"What is written in the Law?" he replied. "How do you read it?"

[27]He answered: "'Love the Lord your God with all your heart and with all your soul and with all your strength and with all your mind'; and, 'Love your neighbor as yourself.'"

[28]"You have answered correctly," Jesus replied. "Do this and you will live."

[29]But he wanted to justify himself, so he asked Jesus, "And who is my neighbor?"

[30]In reply Jesus said: "A man was going down from Jerusalem to Jericho, when he fell into the hands of robbers. They stripped him of his clothes, beat him and went away, leaving him half dead. [31]A priest happened to be going down the same road, and when he saw the man, he passed by on the other side. [32]So too, a Levite, when he came to the place and saw him, passed by on the other side. [33]But a Samaritan, as he traveled, came where the man was; and when he saw him, he took pity on him. [34]He went to him and bandaged his wounds, pouring on oil and wine. Then he put the man on his own donkey, took him to an inn and took care of him. [35]The next day he took out two silver coins and gave them to the innkeeper. 'Look after him,' he said, 'and when I return, I will reimburse you for any extra expense you may have.'

[36]"Which of these three do you think was a neighbor to the man who fell into the hands of robbers?"

[37]The expert in the law replied, "The one who had mercy on him."

Jesus told him, "Go and do likewise."

This parable's unique preaching window to postmoderns

The postmodern worldview is shaped by a belief that pluralism is the model for how life in a multicultural, multireligious, and multiethnic world is best lived. Even so, racism and phobias of all kinds continue to plague contemporary societies. This parable is without equal in laying out for people of all ages—premodern, modern, and postmodern—what loving God looks like in practical, everyday living.

Position of the parable within the text

Luke positions this parable toward the beginning of the travel narrative in which Jesus sets out for Jerusalem (9:51), his arrival some time later marked by his triumphal entry (19:28). Just verses before this parable Luke positions the story of Jesus' sending his disciples into a Samaritan village, after which the disciples, angry because the Samaritans rejected them, ask Jesus to call down fire on the village (9:52-56). Jesus responded by rebuking the disciples, which helps condition our feelings about Samaritans.

More specifically, this parable emerges out of a conversation Jesus has with a "lawyer" or an "expert of the law," sometimes called a "scribe" (one trained to interpret Hebrew law). The interaction Jesus has with this expert provides the framework for the parable and alerts us to Jesus' lesson.

Word study

The Road between Jerusalem and Jericho. There is symbolic significance in Jesus' choice to locate the story between the cities of Jericho and Jerusalem. Jerusalem, the city of worship, was where the priests spent their time serving in the temple. Jericho, a suburban-type community, was where priests often lived, traveling to Jerusalem to perform their duties. King Herod built his magnificent summer palace there; its springs made it known as the "City of a Thousand Palms."

Jericho is first mentioned in Scripture in the account of the children of Israel when they moved from the east side of the Jordan River to take the "promised land." After Jericho was taken, Joshua condemned the city: "Cursed before the LORD is the man who undertakes to rebuild this city, Jericho" (Jos. 6:26).

The road between Jericho and Jerusalem is a lonely seventeen-mile stretch with Jerusalem at 2,700 feet above sea level and Jericho at 820 feet below sea level, a drop of 3,520 feet. This road was notorious for its robberies and became even more dangerous when Herod laid off forty thousand construction workers, leaving plenty of unemployed, some of whom turned to thievery. Five miles above

Jericho was a particularly treacherous pass called in Arabic *tal 'at el-damm*, or the Ascent of Blood, a road perched on the edge of sharp canyons and hairpin curves (Jones, 300).

A Silver Coin. A single silver coin was a denarius, a single day's wage for a laborer.

Cultural factors

Priests. These were members of the tribe of Levi. Under Herod they lost power to choose who would become the high priest. The Romans chose the high priest, often from the party of Sadducees, who were more willing to become political allies with Rome. Under the Romans the political power of the high priest increased. He became president of the Sanhedrin (the city council of Jerusalem) and had the power to levy taxes. Even though they lost power to choose who would be the high priest, they became adept at using their position for personal gain without regard for the spiritual well-being of the community.

Levites. As descendants of the house of Levi, Levites were part of the priestly community. Their role was to assist the priests in preparing the animals, birds, and grain for sacrifices, but they could not take part in the offering itself, on the pain of death (Num. 18:3). They also served as musicians, janitors, and temple police, keeping out those who were disallowed, including the Samaritans (*Nelson's Illustrated Bible Dictionary*, 644).

Samaritans. In 722 B.C.E., Samaria, the Northern Kingdom of Israel, was conquered by Assyria. Over time Assyrians populated Samaria with immigrants from their various conquered nations, bringing along their customs and gods. All of this raised in the minds of the Jews from the south (Judea) a belief that those in the Northern Kingdom were pagan. Called Samaritans, they accepted only the five books of Moses, called "The Samaritan Pentateuch," and established their place of worship at the temple in Gerizim (John 4:9) rather than King Solomon's temple in Jerusalem. Viewed as half-Jews, they were rejected as having any continuing place in the covenant of the Hebrew people (Hultgren, 98).

The historian Josephus writes that early in the first century Samaritans entered the temple in Jerusalem and scattered human bones throughout the temple (*Antiquities* 18.2.2). This alone bred in the Jews a loathing of the Samaritans. One could think of nothing that could divide the two communities more than invading and desecrating the most holy of Hebrew sites.

The Mishnah[3] emphasizes the deep divide between the two communities:

> He that eats the bread of the Samaritans is like to one what eats the flesh of swine. (*m. Sheb.* 8:10; Scott 1989, 197)

And,

> For murder, whether of a Cuthean [i.e., Samaritan] by a Cuthean, or of an Israelite by a Cuthean, punishment is incurred; but of a Cuthean by an Israelite, there is no death penalty. (*b. San.* 57a; Scott 1989, 197)

John, writing of the encounter of Jesus and a Samaritan woman, expresses this sense of cultural and faith distance: "For Jews do not associate with Samaritans" (John 4:9).

Subject
How do I love God?

Complement
I love God by loving my neighbor.

The surprise
The despised Samaritan is the one who demonstrates what it means to love God.

Exegetical outline
I.   A lawyer or "expert in the law," intent on testing Jesus, asks him a question (vv. 25-29).
   A.   The lawyer asks Jesus how he can inherit eternal life.
   B.   Jesus asks the lawyer what the Torah says.
   C.   The lawyer answers Jesus by combining two Old Testament texts.
   D.   Jesus tells the lawyer he has answered well.

    E. The lawyer then asks Jesus who is his neighbor.

II. Jesus tells a parable to illustrate how loving God works outside of the temple (vv. 30-35).

    A. A man is robbed on the road between Jerusalem and Jericho.

    B. A priest coming down from Jerusalem sees the man by the roadside and walks on by.

    C. A Levite coming down from Jerusalem sees the same man and walks on by.

    D. A Samaritan sees the same man and helps him.

III. Jesus shocks the lawyer into seeing that sometimes an outsider will teach us what it means to love God (vv. 36-37).

    A. Jesus asks the lawyer who is the true neighbor.

    B. The lawyer answers, "The one who had mercy."

    C. Jesus' final answer is, "Go and do the same."

Homiletical outline

I. There are some questions that call out for answers.

    A. Few questions matter as much as What does it mean to love God?

II. Too often we fail to see the connection between loving God and those in need.

    A. Religious people are prone to believe that keeping the rules of faith is what gets God's attention.

    B. Caught up in religious performance, we ignore the radical essential of Christ's call to serve him.

III. Sometimes it takes an outsider to shock us into understanding what it means to love God.

The big idea

In loving my neighbor whom I can see, I come to love God whom I can't see. And if I love God whom I can't see, surely I can love my neighbor whom I can see.

Material in order of the text

Instead of answering the lawyer, Jesus tells the parable. Note the structure of the pericope. Jesus' technique is to allow the lawyer to lead with a question, and then he follows up with a question. It is only after the lawyer answers that Jesus gives his answer.

The question-and-answer pattern is as follows:
A Question of the lawyer: How do I get eternal life?
A Question of Jesus: What do the Scriptures say?
B Answer of the lawyer: He quotes two texts.
B Answer of Jesus: Very good.
A Question of the lawyer: Who is my neighbor?
   The Parable
A Question of Jesus: Who is a neighbor?
B Answer of the lawyer: The one who showed mercy.
B Answer of Jesus: Go and do the same.

> [25]On one occasion an expert in the law stood up to test Jesus. "Teacher," he asked, "what must I do to inherit eternal life?"

Most likely this was not the first time this lawyer had heard Jesus, a well-known rabbi who often engaged in public debates. Rabbis were not officially appointed teachers but those whose influence grew because of their ability to attract people to their teachings. Within the Jewish community, public debate was the order of the day. So the lawyer, in asking this question, understood Jesus' teaching and, because of his interest to "test" Jesus, may have known what question to ask.

His question is nonsensical: How does one inherit? By being who you are, of course! A son inherits his parents' wealth because he is their son and they give him what they are expected to give according to their cultural rules. He has no control over either. So, for the lawyer to receive the gift of eternal life, as a Hebrew he would need to keep the Hebrew law so that at the time of his death he would continue to be part of those of the covenant and promise (Bailey, *Poet and Peasant*, 35).

It is possible, however, that, being an expert in the Law, the lawyer might expect from Jesus a listing of what laws he was to keep, from which a debate would then ensue.

> [26]"What is written in the Law?" he replied. "How do you read it?"

Jesus begins with what this "expert in law" knows well.

> [27]He answered: "'Love the Lord your God with all your heart and with all your soul and with all your strength and with all your mind'; and, 'Love your neighbor as yourself.'"

Notice that such a text does not exist in the Old Testament. The lawyer has created a synthesis of two texts: "Hear, O Israel: The LORD our
God, the LORD is one. Love the LORD your God with all your heart
and with all your soul and with all your strength" (Deut. 6:5), and "Do
not seek revenge or bear a grudge against one of your people, but love
your neighbor as yourself. I am the LORD" (Lev. 19:18).

It was expected that rabbis would link various scriptures together,
much as preachers do today. Merging these two texts may have been
original with Jesus or it may have come from another rabbi. It is,
however, quite possible that this expert in the Law, because he may
have heard Jesus refer to it in an earlier discussion, gave a response
he knew Jesus would affirm.

> [28]"You have answered correctly," Jesus replied. "Do this and you
> will live."

This might have ended the conversation if all the lawyer was interested in was in finding eternal life. He does not leave Jesus alone with
this answer, however, but moves into a new arena of conversation by
asking, "Who is my neighbor?" Jesus follows on and broadens the
conversation beyond eternal life to life itself, now and after death.
The verb "do" "is a present imperative meaning 'keep on doing'"
(Bailey, *Through Peasant Eyes*, 38).

> [29]But he wanted to justify himself, so he asked Jesus, "And who is
> my neighbor?"

Luke explains the lawyer's motive in asking the question in the
first place. The debate was in public and the lawyer would want his
colleagues to respect him. He may have assumed that Jesus would
respond with "Your family and friends," to which the lawyer could
easily say, "Those I already do," and walk away with a smile, having
won the argument (Bailey, *Through Peasant Eyes*, 39).

> [30]In reply Jesus said: "A man was going down from Jerusalem to
> Jericho, when he fell into the hands of robbers. They stripped
> him of his clothes, beat him and went away, leaving him half
> dead."

The robbers may have been Bedouin bandits, using their knowledge
of the land to their advantage. Or they may have been Zealots—

with one objective, to rid Israel of foreigners—who, like all freedom fighters, needed money to further their causes.

The story builds expectation that someone will arrive and solve the tragedy. We never learn, however, the robbed man's identity; we know nothing of why he was walking that road, his village of origin, or anything about him as a person, although the crowd would have assumed he was Jewish. Because his identity was stripped from him, those passing by knew nothing of his social or economic status nor his place of origin, which they would have known by his clothes. Neither can he speak. The region was filled with many languages and dialects and one would quickly identify the ethnicity or village of a person just by his or her speaking. The robbed man is indeed anonymous (Bailey, *Through Peasant Eyes*, 42).

To be "half dead" meant that it appeared as if he might be dead, which concerned the priest and Levite. Not only would they be cautious of touching the blood of another—thus creating problems associated with being "unclean"—if the person was dead, just to be within six feet of him would precipitate uncleanness. For the priest, Levite, or Samaritan—all governed by the same religious code—to see someone they thought might be dead would be enough to make them cautious of getting involved.

> [31]"A priest happened to be going down the same road, and when he saw the man, he passed by on the other side."

The priest, one might well assume, had finished his Sabbath duties in Jerusalem and was returning to his home in Jericho. Many of the priestly family—including the Levites—often made their homes in Jericho, traveling the seventeen miles to Jerusalem, living there during their two-week tour of service, and then returning to Jericho. If the priest became "unclean" he must return to Jerusalem, stand by the Eastern Gate with the unclean, and go through the process of purification. This ritual would not only take time, but it would result in a loss of wages. He would have to buy and offer a red heifer, which would take up most of a week and be of significant cost to him, his family, and his household (Scott 1989, 195; Young, 106; Jones, 301; Bailey, *Through Peasant Eyes*, 45).

This matter of ritual purity was critical for the workings of the priestly community. The law stated clearly that

"A priest must not make himself ceremonially unclean for any of his people who die, [2]except for a close relative, such as his mother or father, his son or daughter, his brother, [3]or an unmarried sister who is dependent on him since she has no husband—for her he may make himself unclean. [4]He must not make himself unclean for people related to him by marriage, and so defile himself." (Lev. 21:1b-4)

And:

"He must not enter a place where there is a dead body. He must not make himself unclean, even for his father or mother." (Lev. 21:11)

However, the Mishnah gives a slightly different slant on the subject, giving space for the priest to assess his response.

A high priest or a Nazarite may not contact uncleanness because of their [dead] kindred, but they may contact uncleanness because of a neglected corpse. If they were on a journey and found a neglected corpse, R. Eliezer says: The high priest may contact uncleanness but the Nazarite may not contact uncleanness. (m. Nazir 7.1; Scott 1989, 195)

Because the priest does not know if the person is dead or only in need of physical help, he does not know what to do. If he knew the robbed man was alive, he would be obliged to offer help, for the "saving a life overrides any other prescript of the law" (Hultgren, 97). However, he makes every attempt to avoid the man in need. The Greek verb indicates that he went as far away as possible. His sense of self-preservation takes over and he decides to "take the halakic fork in the road that says he should not defile himself, and so he passes by" (Hultgren, 97).

[32]"So too, a Levite, when he came to the place and saw him, passed by on the other side."

In a sense, these two continue what the robbers had begun in destroying the man. The Levite, following after the priest, would know that the priest had avoided helping the man. Because he was under the same regulations of purification, it is not surprising that if he knew the priest had passed ahead of him, he might have reasoned, "If the priest saw it best to pass by, I had better do the same."

Those of the priestly world listening would applaud what the two did. For either of them to go into the ditch for a person they didn't know and make themselves vulnerable to a lengthy cleansing process would have been seen as nothing less than foolhardy. These two, other priests would conclude, were worldly-wise.

For a commoner, it wasn't as cut and dried. Some would want to keep a high view of the priestly community while others would be influenced by a decided anticlerical mood of the day. Those who did would judge the character of these two religious leaders as violating their religious tradition and improperly interpreting the Torah.

> [33] "But a Samaritan, as he traveled, came where the man was; and when he saw him, he took pity on him."

The story turns. Listeners anticipated that three people would face this dilemma. Now that the priest and Levite have come and gone, they expected a Jewish layman to arrive and solve the problem. "The Samaritan's insertion into the story as its hero, the one who helps, shatters the hearer's expectation" (Scott 1989, 198).

And what does the Samaritan do? He feels pity. The noun describing his feelings is "entrails" or "innards," from the Greek *splanchnon*, meaning that his pity grabbed him in the innermost part of his life. As we would use "heart" today, they described deep feeling by referring to their "entrails" (Hultgren, 99).

But what about the man in the ditch? If he was conscious, what would have gone through his mind watching a Samaritan bending over him, cleansing his wounds and picking him up, setting him on his donkey? What would have been his thoughts as he was carried into the nearest village, possibly Jericho, in sight of his colleagues, being cared for by someone from the most despised of communities?

> [34] "He went to him and bandaged his wounds, pouring on oil and wine. Then he put the man on his own donkey, took him to an inn and took care of him."

Instead of stopping with "he took pity on him," Jesus continues, giving a detailed description of what the Samaritan does. "From a literary perspective it allows an audience a longer narration to absorb and put together the unexpected appearance and action of the

Samaritan, a hearer receives a chance to reorder the order in light of this change in order" (Scott 1989, 199).

Wine was used as a disinfectant to cleanse the wounds, oil was used in the ancient world as a curative. The irony is that both wine and oil were used in worship in Jerusalem. The priest and Levite—the very ones with a supply—made no attempt to use in practical life what was used in worship. Instead, it is the despised Samaritan who takes these elements of worship and applies them to the broken and bleeding Jew.

Kenneth Bailey notes there is no evidence of an inn—as we might know it—located out in the middle of the desert. The "inn" was a simple square enclosure at the side of road, provisioned with straw for sleeping, water for drinking, and small enclosures where a weary traveler could stable animals overnight (Jones, 304). It is more likely that the Samaritan would have had to take the wounded man on into Jericho.

> [35]"The next day he took out two silver coins and gave them to the innkeeper. 'Look after him,' he said, 'and when I return, I will reimburse you for any extra expense you may have.'"

Given that a single silver coin was equivalent to a day's wage, the two coins would cover the cost of caring for the wounded man for up to a week (Hultgren, 99). Not only has the Samaritan saved the man's life, but by making the commitment to pay any extra costs, he keeps the man from being arrested for debt. The Samaritan risked his money and, because he was willing to be found with a brutally attacked Jew, he showed his sense of neighborliness, including his willingness to be falsely accused.

The story makes clear the contrast: The robbers beat the traveling man; the Samaritan cleansed and salved his wounds. The robbers robbed him for their own profit; the Samaritan saw to the man's welfare at his own expense. The robbers left him half dead; the Samaritan left him well. The priests walked by on the other side; the Samaritan put his arms around him. The priests left untouched the healing elements of oil and wine; the Samaritan, a layperson, took the elements of worship and used them as the means of healing. The priests avoided the blood and apparent death to avoid being unclean; the Samaritan waived his concern so as to bring cleansing and life. Both robbers and priests avoided mercy; the Samaritan, who knew nothing of mercy from the Jews, was the one who exercised mercy.

> [36]"Which of these three do you think was a neighbor to the man who fell into the hands of robbers?"

Jesus gives no room for the lawyer to escape. He demands that he say what everyone knows but no one is prepared to admit, "the Samaritan." All along the lawyer knew where he fit into the story and that Jesus had him cornered. In his opening question he expects that he will be able to win this debate. His testing Jesus left him with nowhere to turn. There are no further questions he can ask either to extend the conversation or to turn it to his advantage. His protestations of understanding the great commandment, even to the extent that he could draw the two Old Testament verses together, falls flat as he comes face-to-face with his own hypocrisy.

But there is another aspect to the lawyer's dilemma. By bowing to the logic and irresistible wisdom of Jesus, he is implicitly admitting that the Samaritan can keep the law better than he can. He goes beyond admitting his defeat and is forced to accept Jesus' final response, which is more than an answer—it becomes a command. The lawyer knows where the conversation is leading; he is trapped by the rabbi himself, an admission he would not have made minutes earlier.

> [37]The expert in the law replied, "The one who had mercy on him."

Note that the lawyer cannot find it in himself to say "Samaritan," but rather, "the one who showed mercy." Why? Because the Samaritan performed the responsibilities that those assigned by the Law had failed to do and by so doing becomes both a hero and a model for neighborliness.

> Jesus told him, "Go and do likewise."

Jesus introduces a new element to his parables by using the didactic form, "which transforms the parable into an exemplary story. It is a moral tale with a specific focus, rather than a parable proper. Its wider import for the Samaritan mission is that Samaritans, far from being excluded from the covenant of grace, are as capable of fulfilling the Law of God as their priestly Jewish counterpart—and sometimes do it better" (Shillington, 42).

Jesus refuses to give the lawyer a list of how one is to love God. Performance is not an essential of faith. Loving God is.

Homiletical considerations

1. The challenge in preaching this parable to any audience is its overfamiliarity. The ad nauseam use of this as a metaphor—for being kind or good—diminishes its power. The "hook" is to link loving one's neighbor to loving God. While the universal acceptance of this parable as a paradigm of neighborliness gives the preacher an advantage, the sermon must move quickly in building on its reputation and acceptance to show how loving God and loving one's neighbor are inseparably connected. While the story itself does not include God, its does answer the lead-in question, How do I inherit eternal life? By loving God and as I learn to love God I learn to love my neighbor.

2. Today's listeners do not understand the deep hatred people then had for outsiders, believing that no one outside of their ethnic and national clan had any right to the coming messiah's kingdom. The preacher needs to find ways to make this underlying hatred obvious.

3. This parable, by its overfamiliarity, can easily become saccharine with the usual "Love your neighbor" theme. So how does one preach this parable with freshness? The presence of the Samaritan—when properly told—shocks religious people into realizing how often they get caught up in the particularities of their faith, forgetting that loving their neighbor is the foremost factor in loving God.

4. Rather than the lesson of the parable being only about loving one's neighbor, the opening and closing interchange between the lawyer and Jesus are critical and instructive. The lawyer asks about living life eternally and Jesus presses him to Scripture to learn what it says. The question that emerges is, What is the essential element of the text? It is to love God with everything at our disposal. That is the great law. Loving our neighbor, though critical, follows the first. The question Jesus answers is, How does one go about loving God? It is in trying to answer that question that the parable's purpose emerges. To love God is expressed in loving others, and in loving others one comes to love God. Or, in the words of the big idea, "In loving my neighbor whom I can see, I can learn to love God whom I can't see." And conversely, "If I can love God whom I can't see, surely I can love my neighbor whom I can see."

5. In preaching this parable, the story needs to be retold with sufficiently fresh material to intrigue the audience. After the story is told, let the audience see the major movements and how they are pulled together in the big idea.

6. While the lawyer expected the third person to be a Jewish commoner, or at least a Jew of his background who does good, Jesus does not give such an opportunity. Instead, he pulls into play someone who symbolizes not just what the listener deeply hates and rejects but a people who in the view of the teachers of the Law had no right to the coming kingdom.

7. The major movements in this parable are:

a.   Jesus responds to the lawyer's question by answering what loving God looks like in everyday living.

b.   The second movement is to open up the story to the shocking realization that at times those we think are less likely to love God are those who do, while those whom we think are the real God lovers, show by not loving others how they do not love God.

c.   The third movement is in Jesus' command to do the same. Here the application to Monday is critical.

Parable Six:
The Friend at Midnight (Luke 11:1-13)

Text

¹One day Jesus was praying in a certain place. When he finished, one of his disciples said to him, "Lord, teach us to pray, just as John taught his disciples."

²He said to them, "When you pray, say:

"'Father,
hallowed be your name,
your kingdom come.
³Give us each day our daily bread.
⁴Forgive us our sins,
for we also forgive everyone who sins against us.
And lead us not into temptation.'"

⁵Then he said to them, "Suppose one of you has a friend, and he goes to him at midnight and says, 'Friend, lend me three loaves of bread, ⁶because a friend of mine on a journey has come to me, and I have nothing to set before him.'

[7]"Then the one inside answers, 'Don't bother me. The door is already locked, and my children are with me in bed. I can't get up and give you anything.' [8]I tell you, though he will not get up and give him the bread because he is his friend, yet because of the man's boldness he will get up and give him as much as he needs.

[9]"So I say to you: Ask and it will be given to you; seek and you will find; knock and the door will be opened to you. [10]For everyone who asks receives; he who seeks finds; and to him who knocks, the door will be opened.

[11]"Which of you fathers, if your son asks for a fish, will give him a snake instead? [12]Or if he asks for an egg, will give him a scorpion? [13]If you then, though you are evil, know how to give good gifts to your children, how much more will your Father in heaven give the Holy Spirit to those who ask him!"

This parable's unique preaching window to postmoderns

A surprising movement among postmoderns is recognizing prayer as being a legitimate part of one's life. Praying no longer is seen as irrational: Prayers of major world religions are recited at public events; books on prayer are hot sellers. This question asked of Jesus about learning to pray fits within the wider religious views espoused by a postmodern society.

Position of the parable within the text

A question by the disciple is the launching pad of this parable: Would Jesus teach them to pray as John the Baptist had taught his disciples? Jesus responds and then, along with providing a model prayer, tells the parable of a friend in need.

In Luke, the difference between the messages of John and Jesus (7:18-33) is obvious: John's message was "largely a matter of placing oneself in a position of ethical, religious, and political uprightness so that membership in the coming kingdom could be insured" (Capon 1988, 69). Jesus steps outside of John's ethical framework and points to a kingdom message of grace, the only way one can meet God's standards.

In the first word of his prayer—"Father"—Jesus makes it known that his message is not that of John the Baptist. He speaks to the God of creation as one would chat with one's earthly father. Even though Jesus is still some distance from Calvary—crucifixion and resurrection—he lets his disciples know that they can pray to the "Father" because they know the Son (Capon 1988, 70).

Leaving aside the expected request for wisdom, Jesus, without reference to higher ideals of spiritual life, prays for the bread of the day. (Surprisingly, only three verses earlier he censured Martha for her preoccupation with such.) Then, Jesus spends the major portion of the prayer dealing with the power of forgiveness, for in canceling another's debt, one gives up rightful ownership to that debt.

Jesus continues: "And lead us not into temptation." What is the biggest temptation? It is to go it on our own; to reject the way of Christ, believing instead that God accepts us when we measure up—as by John's ethical requirements. With that as the prologue, Jesus tells a parable of the Friend at Midnight.

Word study

Scorpion. A scorpion is "a small crawling animal which looks like a flat lobster" and lives in the desert, hiding under rocks. When its appendages are folded in, it can look like an egg, but its painful and poisonous sting can bring death (*Nelson's Illustrated Bible Dictionary*, 62).

Friend. The word is used four times, suggesting that friendship is critical to the understanding of this parable.

Anaideia. This can be interpreted "persistence" or "shamelessness," for *boldness* is viewed differently by various scholars. There are two conflicting views in interpreting this work. Bailey argues that the man requested to help is the one who has *shamelessness*: The reason he gets up to help his neighbor is that he wants to avoid the shame that would come to him if he refused help (Bailey, *Poet and Peasant*, 121).

Hultgren disagrees: The word does not mean avoidance of shame but corresponds to the Hebrew word *chutzpah* meaning "determined persistence," "raw nerve," "brazen tenacity," "bold perseverance," or even "impudence," meaning to be without "modesty" or "respect." This is the only time it appears in the New Testament (Donahue 1988, 187; Hultgren, 226, 231).

Bread. Bread was not only a food staple but also an instrument in the dining ritual. At the beginning of the meal each person would be given a loaf of bread; torn-off pieces were used for dipping up the food (Bailey, *Poet and Peasant*, 123–24).

Cultural factors

Within Palestinian communities there were built-in expectations requiring people to help each other. So integral was this bond to ongoing village life that Jesus in this parable did not need to comment. The honor of the village was at stake and no self-respecting villager would let his friend, and thus the entire village, down (Bailey, *Poet and Peasant*, 120–21). So, when a guest arrived at a house, even if in the middle of the night, the host was responsible for setting out a meal larger than the visitor could eat (Herzog, 200).

To the opening rhetorical question—suppose one of you has a friend to whom he goes for help?—first-century Jews would answer, "Of course, he will get out of bed and help him." It was inconceivable that a neighbor would object to helping his neighbor in his predicament.

Those listening might very well react: "Indeed, it is an honor, not an annoyance, to be asked to contribute to an occasion that maintains the honor of the village; in doing so, the participants enhance the reputations of their families" (Herzog, 201).

Underlying Middle Eastern views of finances was "the moral economy of the peasant," a belief that peasants had a right to a guaranteed subsistence. Any form of exploitation was seen within that sense of moral obligation, resulting in a trade-off on what was forced on them against what they gained by way of guarantee (Scott 1989, 85–87).

The village was where peasants found equity and justice. Anything that threatened its well-being or stability would be resisted. When a villager asked another for help, that person was obligated by the very nature of relationships within the village to help. To think otherwise would destroy what was essential for their collective existence (Herzog, 205). In this parable one sees evidence of "the extravagant hospitality of the village and . . . the code of honor that sustains it" (Herzog, 207).

Subject
How does God want us to pray?

Complement
God wants us to be unrelentingly persistent in our prayers.

The surprise
God wants us to be persistent, demanding his attention with "shameless boldness" (Donahue 1988, 187). God is seen as human. While in other parables God is pictured as a loving father or a persistent and caring shepherd, here God is seen to encourage an unrelenting persistence in demanding to have one's needs met. By seeing God in this way, one better understands what God expects of those who pray.

There are two ways one may read this text. One is that the person in need is central. Another is that the one being asked to help is central. Joachim Jeremias understands the parable not as if the neighbor is refusing the request, "but rather the utter impossibility of such a refusal" (Jeremias 1972, 158).

> Can you imagine that, if one of you had a friend who came to you at midnight and said to you, "My friend, lend me three loaves, because a friend has come to me on a journey and I have nothing to set before him," you would call out, "Don't disturb me . . . "? Can you imagine such a thing? The answer would be—'Unthinkable!' Under no circumstance would he leave his friend's request unanswered. (Jeremias 1972, 158)

To hear the parable through the voice of the one being asked speaks of God's generosity and not—as in the traditional interpretation—as though God seems grumpy and reluctant to meet the needs of his asker.

While this interpretation keeps the listener from seeing God as "grumpy," it does not do justice to the message of the entire section (vv. 1-13), which is the person's role in praying. Jesus is clearly telling the disciples that they are to ask in time of need, they are to be persistent and be determined in asking, believing that underlying the prayer is a loving Father.

The traditional interpretation is consistent with the entire pericope, including Jesus' promise that if fathers know how to give to their children, how much more the heavenly Father is willing to give the Holy Spirit.

This later reference to the Holy Spirit is a surprise: Why does Jesus include the Spirit in this lesson on praying? Within his two writings—the Gospel according to Luke and the Acts of the Apostles—Luke shows a continuing interest in the work of the Holy Spirit, who provides words when needed (Luke 12:12) and makes the people of God bold for witness (Acts 2:17-18; 4:8, 29-31). Luke points out that the Father—by giving the Holy Spirit to those who ask—helps God's children to pray by the Spirit.

Exegetical outline

I. Jesus teaches the disciples about prayer (vv. 1-4).
   A. He gives them a model of how to pray.
II. Jesus illustrates the nature of prayer with a parable (vv. 5-8).
   A. A man has a problem: A friend has arrived in the middle of the night.
   B. To solve his problem the man has to wake up a neighbor.
   C. After listing objections, the neighbor gives what is asked for.
III. Jesus instructs us how to go about praying (vv. 9-12).
   A. As we pray we are to increase the intensity.
   B. Praying requires that we stay at it.
   C. In praying, we are to see God responding as we would to a son.
IV. God the Holy Spirit works alongside us as we pray (v. 13).
   A. The Holy Spirit enables us in speaking faith.

Homiletical outline

I. Prayer is a learned task (vv. 2-4).
   A. At the heart of prayer is a relationship with the Father.
   B. God is concerned about the mundane and the essentials of life.
   C. While God meets our obvious needs, he wants us to be conscious of wholesome relationships with others.
II. God wants us to be up-front about our needs (vv. 5-8).
   A. In the most impossible of times, be persistent with God.
   B. When objections seem to block the way to answered prayer, keep on.

III. Prayer operates on the basis of faith (vv. 9-13).
- A.   Whether or not we think this approach is too much based on human initiative, persistence is required.
- B.   By its nature, faith takes the promise seriously, even to the point of failure.
- C.   Our heavenly Father won't give substitutes.
- D.   We can count on God, by the Holy Spirit, to help us pray.

The big idea

God wants us to be unrelentingly persistent with our requests.

Material in order of the text

> [5]Then he said to them, "Suppose one of you has a friend, and he goes to him at midnight and says, 'Friend, lend me three loaves of bread, [6]because a friend of mine on a journey has come to me, and I have nothing to set before him.'"

"Suppose one of you" is used for the first time here in Luke and is a way of introducing a parable (see 11:11; 15:4; 17:7). "Midnight" is a way of saying the visitor arrived sometime "in the middle of the night" (Hultgren, 228).

The man's request is not because he seeks something for himself but for a friend who has arrived. He does not have the requisite food to fulfill the strict Middle Eastern code of meeting the needs of a visitor and so he calls out for help. In effect, Jesus is asking, "Suppose you had a friend come in the middle of the night and you had no bread, what would you do? Would you just put your visitor to bed, ignoring the importance of making sure he is fed after the journey? Of course not. You'd do what any self-respecting citizen would do, hustle around until you found food."

> [7]"Then the one inside answers, 'Don't bother me. The door is already locked, and my children are with me in bed. I can't get up and give you anything.'"

The culturally accepted norms would not allow the neighbor to say these words, for each statement implies a refusal:
a.   Don't bother me.

b. The door is locked.

c. The family is in bed.

d. I can't get up.

Bailey notes that a villager would not knock on a neighbor's door late at night, but would call out so the neighbor would recognize the voice of the one calling at such an hour (Bailey, *Poet and Peasant*, 122).

The objection that he would have to wake his children was empty. Peasants lived in one-room houses. The neighbor's calling would have already roused the entire household, so waking the children by getting up was not an issue. As well, his call in the middle of the night would go beyond the one house, rousing others in the village. The one asked would consider it an honor, not an annoyance, to be asked to help his friend and, in so doing, reinforce the honor of the village. Neither was the opening of the door problematic. These objections are to be seen as trivial and only a means of building up the listener's assumption that the refusing of the request simply will not happen.

> [8]"I tell you, though he will not get up and give him the bread because he is his friend, yet because of the man's boldness he will get up and give him as much as he needs."

While this makes an interesting story, a neighbor in the Middle East would simply accept the inconvenience and meet his friend's need, not only because he is a friend but because of the need to be hospitable.

Here we have one of the only times Jesus gives any internalized feelings of a person in a parable. His thoughts about not doing it are overcome, ". . . not out of honor (friendship, mutual obligation) but out of shamelessness, because he will be dishonored if the villagers discover his friend standing outside begging for what ought to be freely given. He is afraid he will be disgraced in the village. He has done out of shamelessness what he ought to have done out of honor" (Scott 1989, 91).

In a small community, people knew what others were doing and they cooperated in their chores. For example, women baked once a week, cooperating in the use of a common oven, rotating its use. So everyone knew who had freshly baked bread (Bailey, *Poet and Peasant*, 122).

> [9]"So I say to you: Ask and it will be given to you; seek and you will find; knock and the door will be opened to you."

"So I say to you" is a warning that what is about to be heard is framed by divine authority. This homily is at the heart of what Jesus has just said in the parable.

> [10]"For everyone who asks receives; he who seeks finds; and to him who knocks, the door will be opened."

Jesus makes clear the relationship of the action to the response: He establishes an equation between initiating a search and receiving a response.

> [11]"Which of you fathers, if your son asks for a fish, will give him a snake instead? [12]Or if he asks for an egg, will give him a scorpion?"

This rhetorical question links the parable with fathers being kind to their children. Those listening would respond, "Why, of course I would not. What he said is unthinkable."

The implicit message is, "As we as sinful humans wouldn't think of violating our social code by refusing help to someone in need, or by refusing to be kind to our children, so your Father will not ignore you in your need."

> [13]"If you then, though you are evil, know how to give good gifts to your children, how much more will your Father in heaven give the Holy Spirit to those who ask."

This is a "how much more" parable. It works this way: If people will go out of their way to help, imagine *how much more* our heavenly Father will help. In this parable Jesus is implicitly saying, "If this person, inconvenienced as he is in the middle of the night, helps his neighbor, *how much more* will your heavenly father move heaven and earth to meet your need?" Or, "If you as a sinful person will not trick your child by giving stones for bread, *how much more* will your heavenly father be faithful in meeting your real needs?"

Homiletical considerations

1. The challenge in preaching this parable to a postmodern is to move toward the obvious point of the parable, in which Jesus makes

clear the responsibility people have in pursuing God in matters of need. God does not expect people to remain as victims along the walkway of life. Passive faith is not faith at all. While this will not satisfy the question "If God is good, why doesn't God answer my prayers?" Jesus' point is to push people beyond a romantic view of God to the rough-and-tumble world in which God expects an active and persistent faith.

2. The mind can be appealed to in this parable through the assumption that spirituality is both legitimate and worthwhile. This entry brings with it the larger issue of God as father and one who in times of need will respond to our cries of help. Without having to drive an unbeliever to the point of saying he or she believes in God before asking for help, the preacher can lead that same person into prayer and, by so doing, fan the flame of faith toward God.

3. There are two windows through which the sermon may be seen, both expanding on the same issue:
   a. Prayer is the way to get God's attention to meet needs.
   b. Why does God require us to "wake him up in the night" to get God to answer our needs?
The second creates tension and makes clear what many ask: Why must I press God for answers to my needs? If God is God and cares for me, why must I push God to get what I need?

4. Several questions can help in examining one's "need":
   a. Is the request a legitimate need?
   b. Is it a request others would affirm?
   c. Is the prayer based on a dependency for God's help?
   d. Is the prayer based on expecting God's help?

5. There are several ways in which the sermon can be preached:
   a. Begin by telling the parable (vv. 5-8) and then use Jesus' homily (vv. 9-13) as the preaching text. This focuses on Jesus' application, which is to respond to his verbal cue, "So I say to you" (v. 9).
   b. Or, use the introduction to deal with the disciples' request to be taught to pray (v. 1). Then consider the prayer under section 1 (vv. 2-4) of the outline and the parable under section II (vv. 5-8) of the outline. Doing it this way, however, makes it even more important that Jesus' interpretation (vv. 9-13) not be lost.

6. This parable raises the question, If God the Father is so willing to give, why do God's children have to ask? If God delights in giving to

his children, why do they have to go about making the request if God knows even before they ask? It helps the audience to know early in the sermon that this question is not what Jesus is setting out to answer.

Parable Seven: The Rich Fool (Luke 12:13-34)

Text

[13]Someone in the crowd said to him, "Teacher, tell my brother to divide the inheritance with me."

[14]Jesus replied, "Man, who appointed me a judge or an arbiter between you?" [15]Then he said to them, "Watch out! Be on your guard against all kinds of greed; a man's life does not consist in the abundance of his possessions."

[16]And he told them this parable: "The ground of a certain rich man produced a good crop. [17]He thought to himself, 'What shall I do? I have no place to store my crops.'

[18]"Then he said, 'This is what I'll do. I will tear down my barns and build bigger ones, and there I will store all my grain and my goods. [19]And I'll say to myself, "You have plenty of good things laid up for many years. Take life easy; eat, drink and be merry."'

[20]"But God said to him, 'You fool! This very night your life will be demanded from you. Then who will get what you have prepared for yourself?'

[21]"This is how it will be with anyone who stores up things for himself but is not rich toward God."

[22]Then Jesus said to his disciples: "Therefore I tell you, do not worry about your life, what you will eat; or about your body, what you will wear. [23]Life is more than food, and the body more than clothes. [24]Consider the ravens: They do not sow or reap, they have no storeroom or barn; yet God feeds them. And how much more valuable you are than birds! [25]Who of you by worrying can add a single hour to his life? [26]Since you cannot do this very little thing, why do you worry about the rest?

[27]"Consider how the lilies grow. They do not labor or spin. Yet I tell you, not even Solomon in all his splendor was dressed like one of these. [28]If that is how God clothes the grass of the field, which is here today, and tomorrow is thrown into the fire, how much more will he clothe you, O you of little faith! [29]And do not set your heart on what you will eat or drink; do not worry about it. [30]For the pagan world runs after all such things, and your Father knows that you need them. [31]But seek his kingdom, and these things will be given to you as well.

[32]"Do not be afraid, little flock, for your Father has been pleased to give you the kingdom. [33]Sell your possessions and give to the poor. Provide purses for yourselves that will not wear out, a treasure in heaven that will not be exhausted, where no thief comes near and no moth destroys. [34]For where your treasure is, there your heart will be also."

This parable's unique preaching window to postmoderns

The baby boom generation is aging, and with that aging comes a consciousness of mortality even though issues such as personal wealth and health seem to cloud it out. The postmodern mind—often exemplified in the life of baby boomers—works within these two irreconcilable realities. The unique contribution of this parable is to lead postmoderns to the edge of life after death. (A sermon on this parable provides the preacher with an opportunity to follow up in the next sermon on the afterlife.) The focus here is on the inevitability of death and the importance of being smart about how life is lived. Postmoderns struggle between modernity's materialist view in which life is only what we experience in our earthly life over against their growing postmodern instinct that because life includes a spiritual dimension there may something about life after death after all. This parable pushes that instinct and confronts them with the inevitability of death. The inherent tension is between the drive for personal prosperity and pleasure and thinking about death. The importance of this parable is in its ability to help the preacher open a firmly shut window, providing opportunity to speak to the issue of hedonism. The continuing irresistible inevitability of death opens the postmodern mind to see the value of biblical wisdom over against that of their world.

Position of the parable within the text

This parable begins with a request for Jesus to judge a family dispute: A man wants his land partitioned from that of his older brother. Old Testament laws would award control of the land to the older brother (Deut. 21:17). It may have been that the younger brother, unhappy with this arrangement, wanted to divide it so he could work the land alone. Jesus sees it differently; the younger was driven by greed.

The parable is located within the travel narrative, framed by warnings against covetousness (12:15, 21) and followed by warnings about being overanxious about the essentials of life.

In his homily following the parable (vv. 22-34), Jesus gives his explanation: The disciples are reminded how wrong it is to build up material wealth and not consider one's spiritual assets. In his explanation, he warns against hoarding (v. 23): Ravens "have no storeroom or barn" (v. 24c); covetousness and hoarding are examples of not trusting in God. Jesus' call to a radical lifestyle is explicit. His message is that his followers are to trust him for everything and not allow anything to come in the way of that trusting relationship.

Word study

Pleonexia. This word for "greed" (v. 15)—used in other texts of the same time period—means "insatiable" or "excessive," suggesting that greedy persons have reduced themselves to the level of wild beasts or act in such ways as not to hesitate in wronging a neighbor or getting gain by way of extortion (Jones, 145).

Psyche for Soul. The word *soul* is not that part of a person detached from the physical, as if the rich man is talking to a nonphysical part of himself. This notion of the soul being separate from the body— "the immortality of the soul"—was introduced by the Greeks but found no currency in the Hebrew world. Both Old and New Testaments treat the word as meaning the entire self (Hultgren, 107; see Scott 1989, 135).

Barns. Farmers in first-century Palestine stored their grain in a *nubilarium,* a granary or shed located next to the threshing floor, a building large enough to hold the entire harvest (Hedrick, 155). As the grain was threshed—separated from the straw—it would be put in a dry storage bin adjacent to the threshing floor, nearby the family's living space, so as to keep the grain from being stolen.

Cultural factors

Hedrick suggests that this story denounces the upper-class community (Hedrick, 185). Nowhere in the Gospels, however, does Jesus ridicule the rich. In this story, he does not need to; the rich do it to themselves. Their failure to be wise and thus "truly rich" is because of greed. The poor laugh at the rich farmer because of his mistakes.

But why would Jesus tell a story in which the main character makes such basic errors? Why would a successful farmer be caught so late in the growing season with no storage for his extraordinary crop (Hedrick, 159–60)?

The farmer may not have made such mistakes. Because of the difficulty in predicting the final yield, a farmer can only judge close to harvesttime. In the early and mid-stages of growth, the crops might look promising but if there is insufficient rain during the growing period the heads will not fill out. Also, storms may destroy the crop just as it is about to be harvested. Because of many variables in farming, farmers view their current crops in light of average returns over the years.

As well, successful farmers don't count on their yield, even when it is in the barn. They only count it when the grain is sold and the money in the bank. For this farmer not to be ready for an enormous yield is not so much that he was incompetent as that the crop exceeded his expectations. To see the farmer as incompetent layers onto the story what simply is not there. Further, it fails to understand the matter of farming: one year good and next a possible disaster. The preacher must look elsewhere for the key to unlock this parable.

Farmers were warned in Roman manuals written in the early centuries not to overbuild facilities but to build what was appropriate to the amount of land and the history of harvest (Hedrick, 154).

Subject
How do we find true wealth?

Complement
True wealth is found in trusting God and in being generous to others.

The surprise
Jesus is not demeaning success or wealth but is pointing out the false division between wisdom and money. True wealth is being "rich toward God," that is, rich in faith, wisdom, truth, good works, fruits of righteousness. In the end, it took the farmer's death to learn that true riches lie in being rich with God.

Exegetical outline

I. Jesus is asked to judge in an inheritance dispute between two brothers (vv. 13-14).
   A. Jesus tells the man he is not a judge.
   B. Jesus warns the man against greed.
II. Jesus tells the story of a rich farmer who happens to get an unusually large crop (vv. 16-20).
   A. The farmer has a monologue with himself over what he will do.
   B. He decides to tear down his barns and build bigger ones.
   C. He decides to enjoy his bonanza and take life easy.
   D. The man's plans change as God says his life will end that very night.
III. Jesus concludes with a warning to the crowd (v. 21).

Homiletical outline

I. We presume that our wealth is due to our cleverness.
   A. Seldom do we see our lives within the larger world of God's provision.
   B. The arrogance of a secular culture puts stress on human accomplishments.
II. We assume our security is made up in our pensions and savings.
   A. Our society is driven by the need to secure all of life from financial mishap.
   B. As Christians, we have moved a long way from God's call to trust God.
III. "Good living" means enjoying what advertising tells us is the "good life."
   A. Newspapers and news broadcasts are preoccupied with it.
   B. People prepare their portfolios for a life of ease.
IV. There will come a time when we will be faced with our humanity and mortality.
   A. Life does come to an end.
   B. Because of that, today we want to see what will life look like then.
   C. We also want to ask the primary question of the source of our trust.

The big idea

Wealth is found in being wise, not in owning possessions.

Material in order of the text

> [13]Someone in the crowd said to him, "Teacher, tell my brother to divide the inheritance with me."

This parable is told to a crowd of people and is not directed to a particular group, either the Pharisees or the disciples.

> [14]Jesus replied, "Man, who appointed me a judge or an arbiter between you?"

As a rabbi, Jesus had no standing to be a judge; judges were appointed in a particular way. Not only did Jesus avoid being trapped into solving this issue, he made it clear that his mission was not to be a judge.

> [15]Then he said to them, "Watch out! Be on your guard against all kinds of greed; a man's life does not consist in the abundance of his possessions."

A possibly better understood translation: It does not depend upon the abundance of things that a person possesses as to whether he leads a profitable life.

From the beginning of this section—before the parable—Jesus sees the young man's problem as greed. By signaling his interpretation before he gives the story, the listener better understands the direction the parable will take.

> [16]And he told them this parable: "The ground of a certain rich man produced a good crop. [17]He thought to himself, 'What shall I do? I have no place to store my crops.'"

The farmer was an honest man—there is no reason to see him otherwise. He was, it seems, the kind of person who was careful in building up his wealth, each year scrutinizing his operation so as to improve it. He didn't take what didn't rightfully belong to him. He seemed to be a person who operated in a prudent fashion. His problem was that he was driven by what he owned. His greed so linked him to his possessions that it became his identity. He wanted more and more of that of which he already had enough. In the English version, personal pronouns are used five times in his soliloquy: "my crops," "my barns," "my grain," "my goods," "myself."

> [18]"Then he said, 'This is what I'll do. I will tear down my barns and build bigger ones, and there I will store all my grain and my goods.'"

He faced a real problem. "What do I do?" he asks himself. In a sense this parable becomes a debate he has with himself.

Jesus does not call honest production a sin. To manage the fields, sow crops, care for their well-being, and then at the end of the growing season be blessed by good weather is only to live within God's good creation. Psalm 128:2 says, "You will eat the fruit of your labor; blessings and prosperity will be yours." The farmer did not need to feel guilty about his success. Biblical lore suggests that successful harvests were a result of being blessed:

> [35]"They should collect all the food of these good years that are coming and store up the grain under the authority of Pharaoh, to be kept in the cities for food. [36]This food should be held in reserve for the country, to be used during the seven years of famine that will come upon Egypt, so that the country may not be ruined by the famine." (Gen. 41:35-36)

When the large harvest came, he would consider the price of commodities. With the extra-large harvest—likely others had the same—there would much grain and prices would slip. So the farmer might reason that he could make a handsome profit if he stored his extra grain until commodity prices rose.

In his success he asked himself the right question: "What am I going to do?" His options were:
1. Sell the grain immediately—which meant prices would be lower given the glut of grain on the market.
2. Give it away to the poor.
3. Plow it under.
4. Store it.

He chose the last option. But why did Jesus see this as being so wrong? Why would it have been wrong to build more barns if this is the most fiscally prudent way to manage the enterprise? The actions were not wrong; rather, his motives were wrong: He wanted to build further security into his life. He was not judged because of his success but by how he handled it. Jesus' condemnation came not on the basis of the farmer's failure or success but in what drove him. He failed to understand that wisdom, and not material well-being, is the true measure of wealth.

> [19]"And I'll say to myself, "You have plenty of good things laid up for many years. Take life easy; eat, drink and be merry.""

This seems inconsistent with a smart-thinking farmer whose life had been built on work and not self-amusement. But Jesus makes this the center of the story from which the farmer spins off in the wrong direction. His storing of his grain makes perfectly good sense. He is doing what a good farmer does: He protects the gift of God—grain. Then, after being smart and acting as expected, he shows himself for what he is: self-centered.

His consideration of building new barns—apart from facing problems of getting them built in time for harvest—may have been his way of constructing his thinking, to provide for long-term security and live a life of enjoyment. In the end he does not understand that life is a loan. The literal translation is, "This very night they are demanding from you your soul," with the "they" possibly referring to angels (Jones, 149). His life view is Epicurean: "Eat, drink, and sport with love; all else is naught" (Scott 1989, 136–37).

The tragedy is that "he mismanages the miracle" (Scott 1989, 137). His sin comes in two ways: First, he did not see the goods as something to share with others. Second, he was trapped by the prevailing view, that God's provision is based on limited goods—a zero-sum view of life, that if one person does well someone else loses. Believing there is only so much to go around if he shares with others, he loses. Instead of understanding that God's abundance toward one person is not limited if someone else receives in abundance, he never has opportunity to enjoy his success.

> [20]"But God said to him, 'You fool! This very night your life will be demanded from you. Then who will get what you have prepared for yourself?'"

Nowhere else does God say, "You fool!" apart from, "The fool says in his heart, 'There is no God'" (Ps. 14:1). Such "a fool" is one "who rejects the order of the world articulated by the wise, that is, one who refuses to acknowledge dependence upon God" (Hultgren, 107). His foolishness is made even more apparent when God says that "this night" life would end, an unexpected turn from the rich man's earlier expectations of "ample goods laid up for many years" (v. 19, NRSV).

Such an explosive response shocks those listening. There is no other parable of Jesus' in which God's voice breaks in. He uses a word he forbids others to use (note Matt. 5:21-22). What the farmer did not understand was that the fruits of his labor were in effect on loan from the Creator, to be used to benefit creation.

His foolishness, as the psalmist noted, is nothing short of operational atheism. Regardless of his profession of faith, personal belief, or public practice, he lives *as if* God does not exist and that is the core of his foolishness. Fools say, either as a thought-out system of atheistic belief or by the practice of life, that God has nothing to do with what they want, or what they want to accomplish. Personal greed is in effect idolatry, for life is centered on possessions.

Hebrew literature views wisdom as being "true riches" (Prov. 3:16), and to make personal riches the focus of life is nothing but foolhardiness (Prov. 11:18; 13:7; 23:4; 27:24; 28:20).

> [1]I have seen another evil under the sun, and it weighs heavily on men: [2]God gives a man wealth, possessions and honor, so that he lacks nothing his heart desires, but God does not enable him to enjoy them, and a stranger enjoys them instead. This is meaningless, a grievous evil. (Eccles. 6:1-2)

As well, God's judgment of the rich farmer as a fool adds a negativity to the last words of the farmer's soliloquy: "Take life easy; eat, drink and be merry" (v. 19).

In a country populated by the poorest of the poor, such commitment to living the high life would grate on the ears of the poor. While the unusual harvest would suggest symbolically that God had blessed the farmer, that gave him no right to turn that blessing into a self-centered response.

Though the poor would make a natural judgment about this rich man, Jesus does not speak of the person as being mean-spirited, stingy, or ruthless. Though the farmer wanted to amass a larger fortune, apart from his greed there is nothing that indicates he was a bad person. Yet, even with the gain, he is not able by his wealth to prevent himself from being trapped in ignorance—read that as "lacking wisdom"—and the judgment of death.

The farmer ends up misjudging life:
1. He misjudges the extent of the crop.
2. He misjudges the need for more space.
3. He misjudges the years he has to live.
4. He misjudges the nature of true wealth.
5. He ends up with more grain than he can handle and buildings not yet built.
6. He misjudges the nature of wisdom, misplacing it with wealth.

In effect God is saying, "This very night your life will be taken. Then who will get what you've been working so hard to save?"

This is tough talk. See the words dripping with irony. See through this judgment the man's arrogance and ignorance. His assumption that he had years to live was brought to a screeching halt.

> [21]"This is how it will be with anyone who stores up things for himself but is not rich toward God."

Jesus has been telling the disciples not to worry about their daily fare, when out of the blue comes a man who thinks he has been wronged by his brother and asks Jesus to judge. Jesus not only stays away from the issue, he discerns that the issue is more than a justice matter—it is a matter rooted in greed. The man's preoccupation with material wealth is so dominant that he is willing to give up his relationship with his brother and is therefore a fool.

Homiletical considerations

1. The challenge in preaching this parable to postmoderns is to disabuse them of the notion that "wisdom" is best defined by "he who dies with the most toys wins." In the economic "first" world, the entrepreneur has become king. Magazines on successful businesspeople and ideas proliferate on our newsstands. Even though postmoderns are increasingly inclined to include spirituality within their collage of beliefs, in life the market rules and success is defined by materialistic well-being. The shocking end of this parable should be used to alert the hearers into actually believing that wealth is found in being wise and not in being the proprietor of possessions.

2. Because of the powerful drama of this parable, a preacher may be inclined to ignore what triggered it: A young man wants Jesus to

judge an issue with his brother. This needs to be clearly stated in the introduction, which then sets the underlying assumption on which the parable rests.

3. Jesus gives the heart of his parable: He sees the young man asking the question as being driven by greed, pushing to get more than he is legally allowed, which leads to the parable about the force of greed.

4. Dealing with the subject of greed is risky: It is something church attendees know well. The danger is to allow the story to assume that greed is a problem only for the rich. While Jesus often spoke to the poor, the preacher's trap is to let the audience believe the parable is outside of their experience and is only for those thought to be materially wealthy.

5. Thus, the preacher must give special attention to helping the hearers see that Jesus is speaking to their own greed: All persons, regardless of financial means, have "barns" they too want to build, not just because of success but because of the human instinct to hoard.

6. It is advisable not to offer advice to farmers on how they should farm. Most urban congregations know little or nothing about farming, and, further, the agrarian vagaries of this parable are incidental and not substantive.

7. There are four major movements in this parable:
   a.   Greed is an essential issue in living.
   b.   Success has a way of hyping greed.
   c.   The antidote for greed is understanding that God is the source for all of life's possessions.
   d.   Do something that shows that one's trust really is in God.

Parable Eight: The Prodigal Son (Luke 15:1-32)

Text

> [1]Now the tax collectors and "sinners" were all gathering around to hear him. [2]But the Pharisees and the teachers of the law muttered, "This man welcomes sinners and eats with them." . . .
>
> [11]Jesus continued: "There was a man who had two sons. [12]The younger one said to his father, 'Father, give me my share of the estate.' So he divided his property between them.
>
> [13]"Not long after that, the younger son got together all he had, set off for a distant country and there squandered his wealth in

wild living. [14]After he had spent everything, there was a severe famine in that whole country, and he began to be in need. [15]So he went and hired himself out to a citizen of that country, who sent him to his fields to feed pigs. [16]He longed to fill his stomach with the pods that the pigs were eating, but no one gave him anything.

[17]"When he came to his senses, he said, 'How many of my father's hired men have food to spare, and here I am starving to death! [18]I will set out and go back to my father and say to him: Father, I have sinned against heaven and against you. [19]I am no longer worthy to be called your son; make me like one of your hired men.' [20]So he got up and went to his father.

"But while he was still a long way off, his father saw him and was filled with compassion for him; he ran to his son, threw his arms around him and kissed him.

[21]"The son said to him, 'Father, I have sinned against heaven and against you. I am no longer worthy to be called your son.'

[22]"But the father said to his servants, 'Quick! Bring the best robe and put it on him. Put a ring on his finger and sandals on his feet. [23]Bring the fattened calf and kill it. Let's have a feast and celebrate. [24]For this son of mine was dead and is alive again; he was lost and is found.' So they began to celebrate.

[25]"Meanwhile, the older son was in the field. When he came near the house, he heard music and dancing. [26]So he called one of the servants and asked him what was going on. [27]'Your brother has come,' he replied, 'and your father has killed the fattened calf because he has him back safe and sound.'

[28]"The older brother became angry and refused to go in. So his father went out and pleaded with him. [29]But he answered his father, 'Look! All these years I've been slaving for you and never disobeyed your orders. Yet you never gave me even a young goat so I could celebrate with my friends. [30]But when this son of yours who has squandered your property with prostitutes comes home, you kill the fattened calf for him!'

[31]"'My son,' the father said, 'you are always with me, and everything I have is yours. [32]But we had to celebrate and be glad, because this brother of yours was dead and is alive again; he was lost and is found.'"

This parable's unique preaching window to postmoderns

This parable is a stunning story of the unabashed love of the father to expose himself to humiliation so as to prevent the son from being humiliated. While this part of the story has powerful appeal to both modern and postmodern minds, the unique attraction for the postmodern is that patriarchy—and therefore power—is set aside in the interest of the well-being of the fool—the son. Postmoderns, in their antipathy to symbols of power, are attracted to expressions of love in which the mighty choose to set aside their authority for the good of another.

Position of the parable within the text

Luke places this parable after the parables of the Lost Sheep and the Lost Coin (15:3-7, 8-10). Those listening are tax collectors, sinners, Pharisees, and teachers of the Law—the latter who Luke says were muttering deprecatingly, "This man welcomes sinners and eats with them" (vv. 1-2). This introduction clues the listener into the polarity between tax collectors/sinners and Pharisees/teachers of the Law.

Word study

Hired Servant. The term is from the Greek *misthos.* In his speech, the son decides to ask his father to make him into a hired person, distinct from two other options: *dulos* (bondsman or slave) or *paides* (slave, or subordinate of the bondsman). It could be that by asking to be a hired man, *misthos,* he would become independent of his older brother. Such status would allow him to live away from home and earn his own wages, with the potential to gain back what had been lost—thus restoring him, by his good works, back to his family (Bailey, *Poet and Peasant,* 176; Osterley, 183–84).

Dramon. Jesus' use of this word in describing the father running to meet the son "implies straining to the utmost" (Shillington, 156).

The Father and Son. Just whom each one represents is in dispute. Young, who agrees with Tertullian,[4] takes the traditional view, with the father seen as God (Young, 134). Both Barth[5] and Bailey[6] bring a christological interpretation to the father, seeing in the father a representation of Jesus. This is vital for the preaching material, for if the father represents God, then the wider scope of heavenly love becomes the matrix from which love emerges. If Jesus becomes the father, however, then this act is foretelling the act of Jesus in humiliation, rescuing the son from public humiliation.

Pods. Pods—a food associated with the pod of a carob tree—were "sometimes described as the food of the poor" (Young, 145). They were "black bitter berries growing on low shrubs and containing very little nutritional value" (Jones, 218), illustrating the extreme poverty of the younger son.

Cultural factors

Bailey says that no story explodes the traditions and values of the Middle East as does this story, beginning with the younger son asking for his inheritance. The essence to a man's inheritance was land, and the only way it could be received was upon the father's death. Thus, his request was essentially, "Father, I wish you would drop dead." Such language to one's father was unheard of, violating the core of Middle Eastern culture, as it called into question the authority and dignity of the father, the patriarch of the family. "In first-century context, such a major family crisis riveted the listener with the shock effect of unusual events" (Bailey, *Poet and Peasant*, 168; see also Young, 137–40).

According to the Mishnaic law and the Old Testament (Deut. 21:17), the inheritance of the two sons would be divided, with one-third going to the youngest and two-thirds to the eldest. Even though the father might divide the land before his death, he retained rights to the use of the land. This story is complicated in that the younger son, in selling his portion, would leave the father without rights to the land's usage (note Jeremias 1972, 128–29).

The younger son had a problem, not only with his father and brother but also with his home village. His sullied reputation would have reached home: He had sold the land; he had lost his money to Gentiles; he ended up working for a Gentile; he worked feeding swine. So, as he contemplates returning and facing his village, he knows what to expect: the *gesasah*. The *gesasah* was a ceremony by townspeople for a son of the village who had either lost his money to Gentiles or married an immoral woman. They would gather around him, breaking jars with corn and nuts, and declare that he was to be cut off from the village (Bailey, *Poet and Peasant*, 178). "His entry into the village will be humiliating and ruthless as the pent-up hostilities of the village are vented on him for having insulted his father, sold the land, and now lost it" (Bailey, *Poet and Peasant*, 178).

Middle Easterners were socially and psychologically different from Westerners in that they were more *dyadic*—it mattered greatly what others thought and said of them. "For them, the psychological center is not the isolated ego, the individual. It is the family" (Shillington, 145). Quite different from Western individualism, their identity resided within their family. The younger son's departure had been an insult. Acting out of self-interest, he ignored the respect and honor due his father and family by humiliating his family and village by losing money to Gentiles and living a life of sexual promiscuity.

Land was as central to Palestinian life then as it is today. Ownership was not as individualized as it might be seen today; instead, it was seen to belong to the past and future generations. It was their means of living and their source of identity. "Expulsion from the land was not only an economic disaster, it was a social one. It meant loss of honor, broken survival networks, and disintegration of the family unit. The bitterness of Psalm 137 and the rejoicing of Psalm 126 are witness to this emotional investment in land lost and regained" (Shillington, 149).

The son's squandering of land not only humiliated the family but also put their future means of livelihood at stake. "[The family's] honor and place in the village, its social and economic networks, even its ability to call on neighbors in times of need are all at issue. If the family were to lose its 'place,' no one would marry its sons or daughters, patrons would disappear, and the family would be excluded from the necessary economic and social relations" (Shillington, 149).

One might suppose that the younger son went where many other Jews were going: Four million Jews lived between Persia and Rome, and only one-half million Jews lived in Palestine. Often younger sons, unable to make a living on the percentage of land they received in their inheritance, emigrated to look for work in places where there was greater potential (Donahue 1988, 153).

Subject
How can I know God's love?

Complement
I learn of God's love as I turn my steps homeward.

The surprise

The surprise element is found in the cultural shocks and the inappropriate behavior, by not only the sons but the father as well. Nothing in this parable makes cultural sense to the Middle Eastern mind and that is the parable's brilliance: It never stops surprising.

Beginning with the audacity of the younger son, who asks his father for his inheritance ("Father, please drop dead so I can get my money!"), the parable follows up with the older brother doing nothing. The audience would have expected him at least to initiate diplomacy, but that does not happen. The land, the most precious inheritance, is sold, after which the younger son goes off to a Gentile city. There he loses his money, as later is learned from the older son, by running around with prostitutes. Worse, the money is lost to Gentiles, of all people. The younger brother then ends his sojourn feeding pigs.

This is just the opening surprise. What shocks the listeners is the father's response in lifting his son's humiliation—which he is sure to receive from the villagers—by humiliating himself.

Exegetical outline

I.   The younger son of a landowner asks his father for his share of the inheritance (vv. 11-16).
  A. The son takes his wealth and travels to a Gentile city.
  B. He loses his money and ends up hungry.
  C. He is alone, without friends or support.
  D. The only job he can find is feeding swine.
II. The son wakes up to his situation and decides to go home (vv. 17-24).
  A. The son, hungry and broke, returns home to his father.
  B. He prepares a speech of repentance.
  C. He will ask his father to make him into a worthy workman.
  D. His father intercepts him.
  E. The father calls for a party, proclaiming the wonders of a lost son now found.

Homiletical outline

I.   Sometimes we are stupid, ignoring the good with which we are blessed.

A. Bullheaded, we pick up and walk away from what is best.
B. In our stubbornness, we squander our inheritance.
C. We eventually hit the wall, spiritually and emotionally depleted and alone.
D. We end up living in ways we would never have thought we would.

II. Something wakes us up and, if we are desperate enough, we rethink what is important.

A. Our first inclination is to try and undo our mistakes, after which we believe God will love us.
B. We assume the real courage is in admitting we are wrong.
C. After learning what God has done for us, we wake up to the fact that the courage was in his action and not ours.
D. Once we come back to God, we see that even with all of our attempts to build our own reentry to God's grace, God loved us anyhow.
E. What is so amazing is the way we are picked up in God's loving arms and called son or daughter by God, as if we had never left.
F. The surprise is that everything in the Father's house is ours if we only turn our steps homeward.

The big idea

God goes to extraordinary lengths to lift us from our failures and cover our humiliation.

Material in order of the text

Some see the father in this parable as God the Father, and others see him as Jesus the Savior. For purposes of this homily, the former metaphor has been chosen. As well, given the length and two-fold division of the parable, this study is limited to a study of the younger son.

> [11]Jesus continued: "There was a man who had two sons. [12]The younger one said to his father, 'Father, give me my share of the estate.' So he divided his property between them."

In essence, the younger son says, "Father, I wish you would drop dead," rudely defying the patriarch. Here the responsibility of doing something would fall on the older brother, either by demanding his brother apologize or by seeking reconciliation between the two (Young, 141; Bailey, *Poet and Peasant*, 161–69).

When the father gives the land to the younger son, the older son would also have received his two-thirds share. As noted later, however, when the younger returns to the farm, his father seems still to be running the estate. According to Jewish law (the Mishnah), "neither the father nor the son could fully dispose of the land during the father's lifetime" (Hultgren, 74). This lack of consistency between the story and what would have actually happened in real life reminds the listener that Jesus crafted this story for a larger purpose, so that details and consistency are sacrificed for the larger purpose. "The economy of telling a good story need not encompass all the details of the current land and custom" (Hultgren, 74).

> [13]"Not long after that, the younger son got together all he had, set off for a distant country and there squandered his wealth in wild living."

The younger son takes his inheritance—which is the land he has sold—and carries his wealth in a coin currency as described by the New English Bible: He "turned the whole of his share in cash."

"Distant country" is a code word meaning "Gentile country," which adds to the young man's litany of failure and disrespect—who, as a Jew, is willing to forsake the land of his parents and squander his inheritance among the despised Gentiles.

His "wild living" was more than hedonism, it was self-destructive. (In Greek, it literally means "incurably ill.") He was so self-indulgent as to be incurable in squandering his finances in wild living. There was no sense that he had any clue about preserving his capital in order to fund his lifestyle. This kind of self-destruction not only devours capital but also eventually turns on itself, destroying the person (Breech 1983, 192).

> [14]"After he had spent everything, there was a severe famine in that whole country, and he began to be in need. [15]So he went and hired himself out to a citizen of that country, who sent him to his fields to feed pigs. [16]He longed to fill his stomach with the pods that the pigs were eating, but no one gave him anything."

Poverty was not seen by the Jews as necessarily meaning personal failure. But in this case the younger son comes into poverty not only by foolish living but also by losing his inherited wealth to those associated with swine. This linking of a playboy-type living with poverty, swine, and Gentiles implies not only a stupidity and a moral laxness but also a shocking violation of Jewish pride and honor. His inheritance did not last long and neither did his dignity and honor as the Gentile owner saw it more important to feed the swine than his Jewish worker.

The introduction of swine is an obvious symbol of his depravity. Scott notes, "A talmudic curse well summarizes the position: 'Cursed be the man who would breed swine, and cursed be the man who would teach his son Grecian Wisdom.' In this aphorism, swine are equivalent to Gentiles—the same equation that is operative in this parable" (Scott 1989, 114).

Being in need was a new experience for this young man: Not only does he face the loss of inheritance but a famine has swept the land and he ends up desperate to survive.

> The occurrence of a famine exposed him to externally imposed necessity, completely halting his programme of self-indulgence; now, far from being able to have whatever he wanted for himself, he begins to want the means simply to survive. Unless he can overcome this "want," living according to his "wants" would be impossible. The story has shown so far that living out of one's wants not only destroys one's relationship with others, it also destroys one's relationship with oneself. The younger son has not only hardened his heart towards his father, he has now destroyed the very basis he had for his life of *self*-indulgence. (Breech 1989, 192)

Being alone, with no one to care, was for him a new experience. At home he had been surrounded with those who cared. While spending his inheritance, there were plenty of friends as long as he footed the bill. Now that has come to an end. He faces what he has never faced before. In wanting to eat what the swine eat, he becomes one with them and by so doing loses not only his family identity but his identity as a man.

The phrase "hired himself out" literally means he was "joined" or "glued" to a person of means who would give him work. But even so, he was given no food.

> [17]"When he came to his senses, he said, 'How many of my father's hired men have food to spare, and here I am starving to death!'"

It seems his change of heart comes more from a guilty heart. "When he came to his senses" (v. 17) suggests he was ready to return home, repent of his misdeeds, and pay back what had been lost (Young, 146). Other scholars do not support such altruism, reasoning that his return was more from a realization that his life was going nowhere and the options at home were much greater than it was out of a desire to repent to his father.[7]

> [18]"'I will set out and go back to my father and say to him: Father, I have sinned against heaven and against you. [19]I am no longer worthy to be called your son; make me like one of your hired men.' [20]So he got up and went to his father."

It is uncertain whether he understands that his sin is more than against his father, family, and village but against the God of heaven. Even though he seems to see the nature of his failure, he decides to risk village scorn and denouncement and sets out toward home, all the while rehearsing his speech of shame and confession.

His speech is threefold. He first confesses his guilt: "Father, I have sinned against heaven and against you." He admits that what he has done resulted in a destruction of the father-son relationship: "I am no longer worthy to be called your son." And finally he suggests a solution: "Make me like one of your hired men."

He does not say what his sin was—leaving home, wasting his inheritance on Gentiles, bringing dishonor on the family and village. Later on, the older brother expresses his opinion, but in this speech it is not told (continuing v. 20 from above).

> "But while he was still a long way off, his father saw him and was filled with compassion for him; he ran to his son, threw his arms around him and kissed him."

This story is not played out on a North American or European farm. People of all social and economic classes lived together in the village, protected by a common stone fence, and for good reason: There were no armies to protect them from roving bands of robbers. Thus, the father would be in the village when he saw his son approaching. Instinctively, he saw the possible danger to his son: If the townspeople saw the son first they might declare him rejected from the village because of the humiliation he had brought, not only on his own father and family but on the village itself. It is here the actions of the father are instructive: *He ran to his son.*

The proper Middle Eastern response for the father would have been to wait until the son arrived at home, fell on his knees, and asked for forgiveness. Not so here. The picture, rather, is of a father—broken by the loss of his son more than the loss of his land—who never stops looking for his wandering son to return home. There is no sense that he is angry or rejects his son, only that he longs for his son to return. It is here the father seems more appropriately to be a metaphor of God than of Jesus. The blending of the two, within a Christian understanding of the Trinity, allows for the interchange of one with the other. For the Palestinians listening to the story, any allusion to a suffering Savior as represented by the father in the story is quite out of the picture. Those listening would quite readily see God as the father. And though this picture would not be new, it was startling in that the younger son, who had so brutally violated the norms and expectations of his world, was loved with wild enthusiasm.

The father is seen as the victim of his son's self-centered actions. Indeed, earlier he was quite helpless after he had given in to the younger son's request. He had not argued or disputed his son's demands. Yet at the very moment the son appears, the father abandons his own stature in his community to rescue his son from being humiliated by a possible *gesasah*, in which the townspeople would disclaim him and eject him from the town of his lineage and family.

The turning moment in the parable is when the father *runs*. For the father to run, he had to lift his robe, which would humiliate him before the villagers, as men were not to show their ankles. Hultgren notes that, "according to tradition, the 'way' a man walks 'shows what he is' (Siriac 19:30) and therefore a dignified man does not run" (Hultgren, 78). It is here that the story finds its true focus: The father runs, choosing to besmirch his own reputation rather than expose his son to humiliation by the townspeople.

Kissing, too, was a ritual with profound significance. In a public dispute in which reconciliation has been achieved, "a part of the ceremony enacted as a sacrament of reconciliation is a public kiss by the leading men involved." In this case the father "fell on his neck," words reminiscent of the reconciliation of Jacob and Esau (Gen. 33:4). The father, by kissing the son first, prevented the son from doing what he would have been expected to do, and that was to kiss his father's hand or feet. Instead, the father kisses first, thus keeping the son from having to show his father's superiority. (The particular Greek word for kissing can mean either to "kiss tenderly" or to "kiss again and again.") (Bailey, *Poet and Peasant*, 182–83).

> [21]"The son said to him, 'Father, I have sinned against heaven and against you. I am no longer worthy to be called your son.'"

In the rabbinic tradition, repentance was seen as making reparation. "The idea that repentance is a 'work' which man does prior to God's acceptance of him is found through rabbinic literature" (Bailey, *Poet and Peasant*, 179).

The son does not finish his rehearsed speech, however. He is not even able to say "make me like one of your hired men." Whether it was because the father interrupted him, keeping him from completing his request, or because the son saw in the father an overwhelming love, wiping out his plan to pay back what he had lost, is not known. Bailey reflects:

> What are the ramifications of his decision [not to complete his request]? . . . The prodigal comes home with a rabbinic understanding of repentance. He is shattered by his father's demonstration of love in humiliation. In his state of apprehension and fear he would naturally experience this unexpected deliverance as an utterly overwhelming event. Now he knows that he cannot offer any solution to their ongoing relationships. He sees that the point is not the lost money, but rather the broken relationship which he cannot heal. Now he understands that any new relationship must be a pure gift from the father. He can offer no solution. To assume that he can compensate his father with his labor is an insult. "I am unworthy" is now his only appropriate response. (Bailey, *Poet and Peasant*, 183–84)

> [22]"But the father said to his servants, 'Quick! Bring the best robe and put it on him. Put a ring on his finger and sandals on his feet. [23]Bring the fattened calf and kill it. Let's have a feast and celebrate. [24]For this son of mine was dead and is alive again; he was lost and is found.' So they began to celebrate."

The servants are told to dress the son, much as one would "dress" a king or celebrity—not unlike Pharaoh giving Joseph a special robe (Gen. 41:42). By so doing, the father signals to the servants and the townspeople who have gathered that the son of disrepute is to be treated with dignity. The father allows no misgivings or second thoughts on how others are to see his son. By ordering the servants to treat his son with care by first getting a robe—a garment of distinction—and then assisting the son in donning the garment, he gives a clear and unmistakable sign (Bailey, *Poet and Peasant*, 185).[8]

The ring, a bestowal of authority (Gen. 41:42; Esther 8:2), is a sign of the father's honor and wealth entrusted to the very one who has squandered one-third of the family's wealth! Receiving shoes is symbolic that the son is not to be considered a servant but is a "free man" in the father's household (Bailey, *Poet and Peasant*, 185).

The killing of a fatted calf—in contrast to a goat or a sheep—means that it is not a modest celebration but one that the entire community is invited to join in (Bailey, *Poet and Peasant*, 187).

Homiletical considerations

1. The challenge in preaching this parable to postmoderns is its implied metanarrative that there is a universal story which speaks to all people everywhere. While parables are important and useful windows into contemporary culture, there are postmodern assumptions that need to be challenged. It is here that Jesus' parables are so helpful. As compelling stories, they give room for the preacher to imply without having to make a major point. The gospel most assuredly is itself a metanarrative. God is creator and father of all; in response to human fall, God had a plan; Jesus did come and, through him, humanity is given opportunity for salvation, in time and forever. And this story is universal. The preacher's challenge, then, is to bring to the fore the wider story out of the implication of this parable.

2. The task of the sermon is to lift the story into today's world with appropriate application: to move it from Sunday to Monday. As with other parables, however, there is value in hearers learning the story, understanding its cultural nuances, and learning to hear it as first-century Palestinians may have heard it. The preacher needs to balance interest in the story with appropriate lessons for the hearers. In giving sufficient information on culture, word interpretation, history, and local color, the preacher can better see how it may have affected Jesus' hearers.

3. It is helpful to divide the stories of the two sons into two sermons and preach them back-to-back.

a. Because this parable is the extent of the pericope, this sermon will be formed by the story itself. It has such wonderful possibilities in surprising people who believe there is nothing new for them to learn. As well, as people understand the story itself, it provides substance for the Spirit in speaking into lives. In the end, if people hear the parable in fresh and informative ways, seeing its surprises and turns, learning to interpret important clues, this can be instructive, assisting them in understanding how to read and study the stories of the Gospels for themselves.

b. There are three major movements in the parable:

   i. Selfishness and greed lead to losing one's place in the family, bringing hurt and embarrassment to all.

   ii. Eventually, one wakes up to find one's life is a mess and it would be better to return home, even though it may bring sorrow.

   iii. The return to the father's home brings about an unexpected celebration, triggered by the father's love.

Parable Nine:
The Persistent Widow (Luke 18:1-8)

Text

[1]Then Jesus told his disciples a parable to show them that they should always pray and not give up. [2]He said: "In a certain town there was a judge who neither feared God nor cared about men. [3]And there was a widow in that town who kept coming to him with the plea, 'Grant me justice against my adversary.'

[4]"For some time he refused. But finally he said to himself, 'Even though I don't fear God or care about men, [5]yet because this widow keeps bothering me, I will see that she gets justice, so that she won't eventually wear me out with her coming!'"

[6]And the Lord said, "Listen to what the unjust judge says. [7]And will not God bring about justice for his chosen ones, who cry out to him day and night? Will he keep putting them off? [8]I tell you, he will see that they get justice, and quickly. However, when the Son of Man comes, will he find faith on the earth?"

This parable's unique preaching window to postmoderns

Justice issues rate high on the radar screen of postmoderns. While other parables also light people's passion on matters of fairness and equity, this parable has heat like no other. The person of this parable is not only a woman (and therefore greatly marginalized); neither is she only a widow (and therefore defenseless against the male-dominated world of the Middle East). She is a widow with no one to defend her against unfair treatment or to represent her interests. Jesus uses this triple combination to draw attention to the central lesson.

Position of the parable within the text

This parable follows Jesus' commentary on the nature of his coming kingdom, comparing it to the times of Noah and Lot, in which people were oblivious to coming divine judgment. Jesus wonders, As there was little faith in the days of Noah and Lot, will the conditions be the same when he returns?

A few verses earlier in Luke's parable, Jesus—while on his way to Jerusalem—heals ten lepers and then responds to the Pharisees' question about the coming kingdom. Then follows this parable on prayer and faith and a parable about a Pharisee and a tax collector. After telling these parables, teaching the multitudes, and healing, Jesus and the disciples end up in Jerusalem, at which time the faith of the disciples is greatly tested.

The warning of the coming of the Son of Man alerts the hearers that because tough times are coming, his followers need to keep on praying, pressing forward in faith, and believing that in the end God will administer justice.

This parable is not unlike the parable of The Friend at Midnight (Luke 11:5-8).

Cultural factors

Bribery was widely practiced in the Middle East during the first century. If a person was poor and could not pay a bribe, however, he or she would be ignored and would have to protest loud and long to receive justice.

As a single woman, a widow in Palestine was helpless, which makes this woman's actions surprising. The judge, by tradition, would have been a person of piety and justice. Yet in this story he is neither. The twist Jesus brings to this parable is that because of the uncharacteristic aggression of the widow, the judge is pushed to do what his piety should have directed him to do in the first place.

The Greek word for widow means "forsaken" or "left empty," even though the Old Testament laws were specific about protecting widows. Because widows usually would not remarry, they had two options: go back to the family of origin—if their original purchase price was repaid—or remain in the husband's family, which meant they would be forced to take a subordinate role. It was generally understood that the fate of a widow was that she would live out her life mistreated by the powerful and possibly sold for payment of debt even though the Romans had laws designed to protect them.

In Jewish custom, widows were required to wear clothes that reflected their status (Gen. 38:14, 19) and were not allowed to wear jewelry or any kind of ornament (Jones, 327). At the same time, the Old Testament was clear in its law that widows were to be protected:

> [17]Do not deprive the alien or the fatherless of justice, or take the cloak of the widow as a pledge. [18]Remember that you were slaves in Egypt and the LORD your God redeemed you from there. That is why I command you to do this. (Deut. 24:17-18)

And,

> [21]"Do not mistreat an alien or oppress him, for you were aliens in Egypt.
> [22]"Do not take advantage of a widow or an orphan. [23]If you do and they cry out to me, I will certainly hear their cry. [24]My anger will be aroused, and I will kill you with the sword; your wives will become widows and your children fatherless." (Exod. 22:21-24)

Prophets pronounced a strong judgment on those who abused widows. As God protected the Hebrews in Egypt, the society is to go out of its way to ensure that widows, the fatherless, and refugees be given special consideration.

Old Testament prophets were particularly concerned about their treatment:

> [1]Woe to those who make unjust laws,
>   to those who issue oppressive decrees,

> [2]to deprive the poor of their rights
> and withhold justice from the oppressed of my people,
> making widows their prey
> and robbing the fatherless. (Isa. 10:1-2)

> [6]"See how each of the princes of Israel who are in you uses his power to shed blood. [7]In you they have treated father and mother with contempt; in you they have oppressed the alien and mistreated the fatherless and the widow.'" (Ezek. 22:6-7)

Job, considered the earliest of Old Testament stories, categorizes those who abuse widows with those who steal, which in a peasant world was considered one of the lowest forms of human behavior:

> [1]"Why does the Almighty not set times for judgment?
> Why must those who know him look in vain for such days?
> [2]Men move boundary stones;
> they pasture flocks they have stolen.
> [3]They drive away the orphan's donkey
> and take the widow's ox in pledge. (Job 24:1-3)

It is strange that, in this world dominated by men, a woman would be out on her own having to press for her own position, with no male from either side of the family standing with her (Bailey, *Through Peasant Eyes*, 134).

The role of judges was important to the well-being of the community and to the service of justice. Herzog notes, however, an enormous distance between the somewhat rarefied atmosphere of the Torah as the

> ideal and the Torah as an actual law code for determining particular situations. . . . It becomes a tool for legitimation and social control, prescribing and proscribing behavior, and it is also employed to protect the interest of a ruling class. The Torah is translated in these changing circumstances by the production of an oral torah in the hands of a class of scribal retainers working at the behest of powerful ruling class interests and then applied to specific cases by a class of judicial retainers. This is the Torah at work in the parable. When property and wealth are at stake, disputes arise, and when the disputes are complicated by issues of family honor and the threat of a woman out of place in the social order, the conflicts can intensify. (Herzog, 227–28)

Word study

The Judge. Sometimes Jesus chooses a rascal to make a point, and in this instance it is a judge.

In this case, only one judge is handling the case, suggesting that the matter was about money. If it had been about land, three judges were required to rule.

Bailey notes three assumptions the parable makes:

1. The widow is in the right and yet is denied justice.
2. For some undisclosed reason, the judge does not want to serve her, perhaps because she has paid no bribes.
3. The judge prefers to favor her adversary: either the adversary is influential or possibly he *has* paid bribes (Bailey, *Through Peasant Eyes*, 133–34).

As well, she is being denied access to justice because she is being denied access to the court.

1. The judge stalls and stalls, refusing to hear the case.
2. The judge is in violation of the Torah by putting the widow off.
3. This suggests that the stakes may have been high for the judge.
4. Being the only judge (for what reason we can only speculate) it would have been easier to pay off one judge than three.
5. Studies of that age and location show that the wealthy used the court system to their own advantage.
6. It would have been easier for the powerful to persuade just one judge to rule in their favor.
7. If the judge was chosen from the urban elite, the judge may have been in "class solidarity" (Scott 1989, 178) with the "adversary."
8. The Talmud speaks of "village judges when willing to pervert justice for a dish of meat" (Herzog, 227).
9. Possibly the judge wanted to keep this off of the "front pages" of the community paper and avoid embarrassment in front of those he knows (Bailey, *Through Peasant Eyes*, 133–34; note also Herzog, 226–27).

Subject

What does faith look like in daily life?

Complement

Faith is pressing on in prayer and not giving up until we receive God's answer.

The surprise

A woman challenges societal injustice in first-century Palestine and wins.

At first, one might be surprised by the linking of a recalcitrant judge to God. Surely such a God does not inspire trust and ongoing prayer. The issue, however, is not whether or not the unjust judge is like God, but the technique that is used—*from the lesser to the greater.*

Exegetical outline

  I.   Jesus calls his disciples not to quit in their prayers (v. 1).
 II.   He tells them a story about a mean judge and a desperate woman (vv. 2-5).
       A. The judge feared neither God nor any person.
       B. The widow pressed him for help against her adversary.
       C. The judge gives in.
III.   He concludes the story with a message and a question (vv. 6-8).
       A. God will listen to those who do not give up asking.
       B. Jesus asks if there will be faith when the Son of Man comes.

Homiletical outline

  I.   Prayer is essential in our lives.
       A. Prayer is not easy.
       B. It seems too often that prayers are not answered.
 II.   Life is filled with the seemingly impossible questions.
       A. Some circumstances seem immovable.
       B. People who could help sometimes refuse to do anything.
III.   God listens to God's children.
       A. When life seems unfair, do not bow to discouragement.
       B. We are to persist until God answers our call.

The big idea

When faced with enormous opposition, keep trusting in God and use everything at your disposal to get justice.

Material in order of the text

¹Then Jesus told his disciples a parable to show them that they should always pray and not give up.

Luke states the purpose of the parable in the opening line.

> ²He said: "In a certain town there was judge who neither feared God nor cared about men."

It seems this Jewish judge practiced in a town small enough that he could not be distanced from those he served. Even though the Romans ruled, they tended to leave civil judgments to the Jews to decide by way of tradition and the Torah.

The judge is pictured as ruthless, one the Jews would see as ignorant of the ways of God. In the Hebrew community, to fear God is to be just (Lev. 25:17, 36, 43), which is the tradition on which wise judgments are to be rendered (Ps. 111:10). So a person who does not fear God cannot be wise (Hultgren, 254).

In ruling over the legal affairs of people judges were expected to fear God, as made clear in the Torah:

> ⁵He appointed judges in the land, in each of the fortified cities of Judah. ⁶He told them, "Consider carefully what you do, because you are not judging for man but for the LORD, who is with you whenever you give a verdict. ⁷Now let the fear of the LORD be upon you. Judge carefully, for with the LORD our God there is no injustice or partiality or bribery." (2 Chron. 19:5-6)

"This high view of justice makes the behavior of the corrupt judge in the parable that much more despicable" (Young, 57).

Mention of not fearing God appears twice ("who neither feared God" and "I don't fear God") in this brief parable, a warning of its critical nature in the narrative.

The phrases "nor cared about men" and "I don't . . . care about men" may mean he either is afraid of no one or has no respect for others. If it is the latter, the language goes beyond a lack of respect to that of contempt. The Old Testament notion of a judge was that he was to be a person the community trusted to be impartial in decision making. However, here he is the opposite: He is "unrighteous."

Not only does the widow suffer from the initial injustice, the judge to whom she appeals becomes an additional source of difficulty and injustice. It is not told who her adversaries are, but, by the character description of the judge, her problem has increased. And, given her lack of social position, she has no advocate to plead her case before this unjust judge.

Because he refuses to hear her case, the hearers quickly judge him to be one who lacks passion for the task of pursuing justice. It may have been that a bribe had been thrown his way; even so, this judge feared no one, including the adversary, regardless of whether a bribe was offered or not.

The judge can be seen in five ways: (1) as a mean person; (2) as one who does not fear anyone and is therefore willing to take a bribe; (3) as one who is beyond shame; (4) as one who is essentially evil, unable to see the perverseness of his ways; or (5) as an "outlaw" judge (Herzog, 221).

> [3]"And there was a widow in that town who kept coming to him with the plea 'Grant me justice against my adversary.'"

According to the Torah, widows are to command a certain respect, as God is their protector. Not only is the nation commanded not to afflict widows (Exod. 22:22-24), the people are to take care of them (Deut. 14:29; 24:17; 26:12-13; 27:19). Thus, if a pious Jew was to care for widows, how much more should a judge do the same?

This is a life-and-death issue for the woman. If her rights are not protected, poverty and starvation may be her lot. With no male member of the family to take up her concern, she is the only one to force the issue before the judge (Donahue 1988, 182).

We are told neither who the "adversary" is nor the nature of the injustice. It could have been an issue of money, or a lawsuit by her husband's family, or possibly eviction from her home (Hultgren, 254). Though it was unusual to see a woman in court, she is determined to find fairness and justice. With no brothers or father able or willing to help, she must do it on her own.

Her strategy is to become the adversary, to force the issue between herself and the judge. By going directly to the judge and then taking the issue public, she put the heat on the judge by embarrassing him. At the gate of the city, an area dominated by men, she kept coming, speaking out, making herself a nuisance, demanding justice (Herzog, 229).

It is the widow who insists that the Torah rules: She denounces the judge in public and then continues to press him to live up to the requirements of the Law. Herzog points out that she reverses roles by upholding the Law in the face of the judge's abject failure to fulfill his task. "It takes constant repetition and nagging persistence to break through the wall of silence erected to protect the cover story and disguise the truth" (Herzog, 230).

Nothing is heard from the person who created the injustice toward the widow. It could be that the plan was to try and keep it quiet and work out a deal without public knowledge.

> [4]"For some time he refused. But finally he said to himself, 'Even though I don't fear God or care about men, [5]yet because this widow keeps bothering me, I will see that she gets justice, so that she won't eventually wear me out with her coming!'"

Though the judge gives no indication of wanting to serve justice, and even though he puts off making a decision, he eventually gives attention to her case, his inner thoughts made public by his soliloquy.

The widow learns she cannot count on his regard for justice or personal integrity to support her, thus turning the one who is helpless into the person of power.

In the end she compels him to move by the sheer force of her persistence. The word *bother* is the same one used in The Friend at Midnight (Luke 11:7). The verb phrase "wear me out" is from the noun meaning "part of the face under the eyes." The verb form, a word used for boxing, means literally "to strike someone on the face in such a way that he gets a 'black eye' and is disfigured as a result" (Young, 58; Hultgren, 255). The judge fears that if he does not do something, this widow will slander him or hurt his reputation, figuratively striking him so as to disfigure him (Hultgren, 255). Or, as Young renders it, "I will grant her justice lest in the end she comes and gives a blow in the face" (Young, 59).

The widow makes no attempt to appeal to the judge's sense of fairness or his desire to uphold the Torah. Instead, she tests his limits by pushing him to the extreme. He would also know that, as much as he wanted to avoid giving her justice, his ongoing ability to judge was based on reputation, without which he would be ineffective and eventually discarded as a judge.

As he continues to delay, all the while wheeling and dealing to cut a compromise, the widow pushes until the judge decides it is best for him to resolve the case. He knows that if she continues to make it public, the people will eventually support her and he will lose face (Herzog, 230–31; Donahue 1988, 184).

Like most parables, this one has an element of humor: The judge—powerful, independent, and fearful of no one—is harassed by none other than a widow. At first he ignores her but is eventually so distressed by her repeated appeals that he says, "I'd better do something before she gives me a black eye!" The very idea that he, being powerful, loses and she, being weak, wins is humorous and quite preposterous.

Herzog summarizes the woman's situation (Herzog, 231–32):
1. She is without a husband, trapped between a power play by the judge and the complex ruling of the Torah.
2. Her case is hopeless: Everyone knows that a woman cannot beat the system.
3. By refusing to quit, she "blows the cover off the whole [legal] system."
4. Her eventual reward is justice.
5. By her "shameless" action she stares down the barrel of societal injustice and wins.

> [6]"And the Lord said, 'Listen to what the unjust judge says.'"

The parable is over. Now Jesus wants the disciples to hear his application.

> [7]"And will not God bring about justice for his chosen ones, who cry out to him day and night? Will he keep putting them off?"

The first question implies a strong "yes"; the second a strong "no." "If an unscrupulous magistrate will be moved to act justly because of the unrelenting tenacity of a helpless widow, how much more will the one good God answer persistent prayer? If a corrupt judge can be influenced for good by someone of little importance and no worldly clout, how much more can the person created in the divine image pray expectantly to the compassionate God?" (Young, 58).

> [8]"I tell you, he will see that they get justice, and quickly. However, when the Son of Man comes, will he find faith on the earth?"

Jesus first supports the question asked in the previous verse and then turns to the theme of the coming of the Son of Man. Whenever the phrase "Son of Man" is used, it signals that Jesus is about to warn of difficult times of persecution and trouble. So, what can be learned from the widow? Though drawn to her plight with the merciless judge, is it her ingenuity and "shamelessness" that unlock this parable?

The "how much more" phrase in effect is saying, "Even though this unjust judge will eventually give justice to the widow, *how much more* will God give us." In reading the parable this way, the judge represents God, so that the lesson is, "Since even this miserable judge will eventually rule justly, think how much more our God will do."

Another view is that as the widow presses the judge, she knows he will eventually have to rule by the Torah, the law of God. So, when Jesus says, "And will not God bring about justice . . ." it may mean that in life, when people like this unjust judge refuse to rule justly, if one keeps appealing to the Torah—God's rule—eventually the judge will be forced to heed the law of God.

This interpretation suggests that, when faced with injustice, the people of God are to continue to believe in God's law as the rule and push their power systems to come to terms with that law. Faith, in this case, is not in the judge or the system but in the Word of God itself.

Homiletical considerations

1. The challenge in preaching this parable to postmoderns is not to allow the seeming incompatible analogy of the unjust judge and God overturn the rather straightforward message of people's responsibility to press God for answers to their questions. The elements of this story are filled with the enormous unfairness of the widow's situation: She is alone, a widow, and without a defender. While the preacher will want to exploit this sense of marginalization, presuming the outcry of the congregation, this is only the opening. To focus on this is to miss the point. The sermon must crystallize the message on being persistent: "If this woman, so abused, can refuse to be victimized by an unjust judge and presses forward in search of justice, how much more should we pursue a judge who is just in search of answers to life?"

2. This parable is one to preach for those living in tough times. While it has its own humor and provides a major surprise, its message is about one's determination to find answers in the impossible times of life.

3. Be careful, as it can be upsetting for those who think they have mastered prayer. Jesus puts a new spin on prayer: Absent is the gentle, acquiescing type of petition. Instead, he tells of a tough, no-nonsense woman who refuses to cave in. Prayer here is not just a matter of keeping on but a refusing to give in "to the sin of despair" (Jones, 336). In effect, Jesus is saying, "Look at how this powerless woman acted in the face of an uncaring, all-powerful judge. She kept on, refusing to bow to the seeming inaction, pressing her point until she got action."

4. The danger is to allow this story to flaunt the notion that success over one's adversity comes only because of one's courageous spirit: a "think and be tough" theology. While this metaphor describes an indomitable spirit, it is ultimately about trusting God.

5. Audiences in the Western world have difficulty understanding the tragic position women suffered in that day and the amazing repudiation of those cultural limitations that this woman's actions represent.

6. Because this is a parable of prayer, it gives latitude in the sermon to explore the nature of prayer, beyond the picture of kneeling, head in hands, mourning the tragedy of life. Prayer here is powerful.

7. This parable takes on a different tone than that of The Friend at Midnight (Luke 11:5-13). This is not just a "how much more"[9] parable but one that calls Jesus' followers into tough times when they will be marginalized, ridiculed, and bounced around by society, even as Jews felt like outcasts in their own land under the rule of the Romans. The widow pressed society to live by a higher law, even if that placed her life at additional risk.

8. Understanding the nature of prayer is a challenge for each generation—for those who followed Jesus up and down the dusty roads of Palestine and for those who speed along interstate highways. How does one understand God? When God does not answer as expected, what in the world is God doing? This parable, a twin of The Friend at Midnight, helps us better understand the character of God. This parable, like so many others, really is about one's vision of God. By the use of exaggeration, the listener comes to a better understanding of the divine nature (Young, 42).

9. Young notes that this technique of "how much more," familiar in early rabbinic literature, was known as the comparing of "light" and "weighty" sides. On the light side was the example: if the cor-

rupt judge will eventually respond to this woman's nagging. On the weighty side was the comparison: How much more will God answer the prayers of his people? (Young, 42). In this parable, however, Jesus reverses the "how much more" literary technique by describing what God is not like. Because God is so trustworthy, there is no need to be afraid of God's justice or willingness. Indeed, God's desire is to meet God's children's cries for justice.

10. In this parable, bold tenacity is treated as a form of religious piety and godly faith, and even though the widow's perseverance borders on blasphemy, Jesus treats it as being acceptable, as shown when he wonders if he will find such faith when the final days come (v. 8b).

11. Major movements in this parable are:

   a. The circumstance of the widow allows for a parallel drawn to contemporary times: A person is in tragic circumstance. What will she do?

   b. Her actions are endearing to an audience. People love an underdog to win. Play out the determined efforts she makes to overcome her circumstance.

   c. The final movement is to tie this into what God expects us to do in prayer.

Parable Ten: The Pharisee and the Tax Collector (Luke 18:9-14)

Text

[9]To some who were confident of their own righteousness and looked down on everybody else, Jesus told this parable: [10]"Two men went up to the temple to pray, one a Pharisee and the other a tax collector. [11]The Pharisee stood up and prayed about himself: 'God, I thank you that I am not like other men—robbers, evildoers, adulterers—or even like this tax collector. [12]I fast twice a week and give a tenth of all I get.'

[13]"But the tax collector stood at a distance. He would not even look up to heaven, but beat his breast and said, 'God, have mercy on me, a sinner.'

[14]"I tell you that this man, rather than the other, went home justified before God. For everyone who exalts himself will be humbled, and he who humbles himself will be exalted."

This parable's unique preaching window to postmoderns

The attraction of this parable to postmoderns is a rejection of the absolutes by which the Pharisee is defined. His unilateral vision of spirituality expressed by a slavish obedience to a list of mini-laws is at the opposite side of the scale of postmodernity in which a tolerant, multifaith community is preferred.

Position of the parable within the text

Luke places this parable within the flow of illustrations about faith and the predications of Jesus' death. Jesus tells the parable of The Rich Man and Lazarus (16:19-31) with the warning that if people do not listen to God's messengers such as Moses and the prophets "they will not be convinced even if someone rises from the dead" (16:31). In chapter 17 he teaches about his coming kingdom, heals ten lepers, and reviews the abysmal days of Noah and Lot and the importance of people being ready for the day when "the Son of Man is revealed" (17:30).

Preceding this parable Jesus tells the story of The Persistent Widow, who ignores expected notions of a woman's behavior to overcome the reluctance of a judge in her search for deliverance. Then, following this parable, Luke includes the encounter Jesus had with a rich man in which he warns his disciples what they will face in Jerusalem.

Word study

Tithe. Tithing was called for in the Torah.

> [22]Be sure to set aside a tenth of all that your fields produce each year. [23]Eat the tithe of your grain, new wine and oil, and the first-born of your herds and flocks in the presence of the LORD your God at the place he will choose as a dwelling for his Name, so that you may learn to revere the LORD your God always. (Deut. 14:22-23)

If one did not pay the tithe of the produce, for example, what was eaten was considered impure and those who ate it were made impure.

The temple tax was different from the tithe in that it was to show others how devoted the person was and it "fulfilled important prescriptions for maintaining a healthy relationship with the God who called the people into existence and made them a great nation" (Herzog, 179).

Fasting. This was "an act of mourning, penitence or intercession" (Shillington, 28).

Cultural factors

There are four important elements that influence one's understanding of this parable: the Pharisee, the tax collector, taxes, and the temple.

The Pharisee. The word *Pharisee* comes from a Hebrew word meaning "separated one." Pharisees were part of a movement within Judaism whose focus was on studying and knowing the Torah and whose concern was with ritual purity and living holy lives to the Lord (Hultgren, 120–21).

The movement of the Pharisees probably originated during the brutal rein of Antiochus IV Epiphanies when Judas Maccabees and his followers were willing to die rather than submit to Greek idolatry and violation of the temple. A group called the Hassidim—the forerunners to the Pharisees—were faithful and loyal Jews who fought against the oppression and occupation of the Greeks, seeking to lift Israel from the moral depravity of these invaders. The Pharisees were good people; you would not be afraid to buy a used chariot from them!

Pharisees were not always unduly proud or lacking a sincere trust in God. The Pharisees were not crooks; they would faithfully pay their taxes, and quite likely they were faithful to their wives and loving to their children. They were also religious, not always hypocritical (as might be thought), but men whose faith would quite likely be matched by a disciplined life. They would pay to the temple 10 percent of their income (Scott 1989, 96). The "God-living" Pharisees, like their father Abraham, saw themselves as the friends of God (Osterley, 43).

Because a Pharisee is central to the flow and meaning of this parable, one must be careful not to assume that Jesus always thought badly of them or that his relationship with them was always antagonistic. In fact, Jesus was often on good terms with them: Luke tells about him going to one of their feasts (7:36). Showing concern for Jesus' safety, they warned him of Herod's plans, begging him to go elsewhere (Luke 13:31). After hearing Jesus' message on inviting the poor, the crippled, the lame, and the blind to a banquet, a Pharisee was so overjoyed at what Jesus had to say that he broke out with, "Blessed is the man who eats at the feast in the kingdom of God" (Luke 14:15). As well, many of his arguments with them were not unfriendly (Matt. 22:34-35; Mark 2:16-17; Luke 5:17; 17:20; 19:39-40; John 8:12-20). Nicodemus showed great interest in the nature of Jesus' life (John 3:1-2) and when Jesus needed someone to defend him, Nicodemus the Pharisee cooled the crowd (John 7:50-51). And it was none other than a Pharisee, Joseph of Arimathea, who cared for the body of Jesus, providing his own grave site (Mark 15:43).

The Talmud points out various kinds of Pharisees:

1. The "shoulder" Pharisee—who wears his good deeds on his shoulder so the whole world can admire it.
2. The "wait-a-bit Pharisee"—who in effect asks that others wait until he has done a good deed: "I am a good person, just hold on."
3. The "bruised" Pharisee—who would run up against a wall to avoid looking at a woman.
4. The "pestle" Pharisee—who walks about looking down in mock humility.
5. The "reckon-it-up" Pharisee—who is always counting up the good deeds he has done to see if they counterbalance the bad deeds.
6. The "God-fearing" Pharisee—for whom Job was the model (*Sota* 22b).

The Toll Collector. Though the term is translated "tax collector," the man in the story was a "toll collector" (*telones*), a minor figure in the elaborate system of Roman taxation. Toll collectors were more despised than tax collectors. They operated booths along the road and did all they could to cheat people out of their earnings. Because of their visibility, they were known to most who traveled in the vicinity and were deeply hated as they came to represent the entire system of oppression that shrouded the Middle East (Herzog, 173).

Direct taxes were collected by government officials. Indirect taxation was handled by those who got the job by contract (Herzog,

187). The lessee—the person who won the contract—would pay in advance the amount agreed on. He would then work to recoup his investment over the designated period of time in any way he could. Donahue notes that, though tax collectors are given some latitude in the Talmud, toll collectors are viewed in harsh ways (Donahue 1988, 3). The reason they could not be forgiven was that repentance required the repayment of all extorted funds plus one-fifth, along with leaving the trade. But since the toll collector assessed different people every day, it was impossible for him to repay what he had overtaxed. (Note that Zacchaeus was called an *architelonés*, which meant he was a buyer of toll contracts. The toll collector—*telones*— in this parable was a more lowly collector, one who would sit at the toll booth. As a more lowly collector, he might live on a subsistence level, cheating on behalf of his contractor yet always defrauding the public [Herzog, 188].)

To the Jews listening, this toll collector was the worst kind of crook—not unlike a Mafia extortionist—working for the Roman government, collecting money from his fellow Jews, and keeping whatever he could exact on top of what he had pledged to collect. For years he has lived well by skimming off the top of what he paid to Rome (Capon 1988, 179).

Taxes. The burden of taxation for a Jew under the Roman system was high. Besides the temple tax, Jews had to pay Roman poll and land tax, land transfer tax, export and import duties, and, those living in Jerusalem, a tax on houses. In Jesus' time Judea was an imperial province run directly by Rome. The tax would be paid into the Roman treasury.

This toll collector was a low-level sort, quite possibly poor, despised, vulnerable to the hatred of farmers and merchants, powerless, and without honor. Not raising his eyes fits with how most would expect him to act. And because he dealt with Gentiles, he would be considered unclean.

Though he was a Jew, those listening would be surprised to see him going to the temple. That Jesus included him in the parable would have had a shocking effect on them.

The Temple. This is an important feature in the story for it embodies Jewish identity and tradition and stands for the primary means by which the people knew their God. What happened in the temple reflected their history and had an impact on their future.

The temple built by King Solomon lasted a thousand years (apart from seventy years of desolation during the time of the Babylonian conquest) until 70 C.E., when Titus and the tenth legion of Rome left the Temple Mount in smoldering ruins. The temple not only played an important religious role in the life of the people but served politically as well, giving legitimacy to the monarch.

From the Hebrew, *temple* means "house of God." Though Yahweh was transcendent, this was a physical place where the people of God could access Yahweh. It had been built and furnished precisely to remind the people of their covenant with God.

This parable does not take place on the road to Bethel or the desert road from Jerusalem to Jericho but in the temple, and because it does, the God of the temple is central. Being set in the temple is a clue for the listeners, alerting them that it is not only about two men but also about God and two men.

Those listening understood how central the temple was to their identity, worship, and economy. "The temple is the map, the metaphor, that stands for the insiders and outsiders. Since this is a parable of contrast, the temple will map out the contrast. The contrast form does not decide in advance whether the first or second one will be favored, although the temple map surely favors the Pharisee" (Scott 1989, 94).

The role of the temple in the life of Israel went beyond its being the place where they met God, however; it was an important institution—thousands were employed to keep its sacrificial system operating, not to mention the many whose task it was to clean it and care for its upkeep.

The temple also acted as a bank for both the rich and the poor, which gave it enormous power. Its funding sources were first from the collection of tithes and then from taxation. There were three kinds of taxes for the temple: (1) the annual "wave offering," which collected from 1 to 3 percent of the harvest; (2) 10 percent of one's income, which went to support the priests and Levites; (3) a second tithe, which was to build up in the six years leading to the sabbatical year. This meant that up to 23 percent of one's income went to the temple, which does not take into account what was paid to Rome. To be religious and faithful was enormously expensive (Shillington,

23–25). For the Pharisee to say I "give a tenth of all I get" was impressive.[10] Such faithfulness was cause to celebrate this good man.

Subject
Who gains God's favor?

Complement
God commends people who come to God for forgiveness.

The surprise
Assuming that the Pharisee is the righteous one, the listeners are shocked when Jesus shows favor to the tax collector.

The interesting paradox is that the temple—the sacred center and symbol of the holy of Jewish society—is made unholy by the ones who were to be the symbols of temple righteousness, the Pharisees. And, in a reverse way, the unholy one—the toll collector —becomes holy even though the whole Jewish world believes he is the unholy one of the story.

Exegetical outline
I.   Jesus speaks to those who look down on others (v. 9).
II. Jesus tells the crowd a story of two men who go to the temple to pray (vv. 10-13).
   A.   The Pharisee prays about himself.
      i.   He tells God what he does not do.
      ii. He also tells God how good he is.
      iii. He then tells God he is not like the other person at prayer.
   B.   The tax collector takes his turn.
      i.   His body language shows his attitude of humility.
      ii. He asks God to atone for his sins.
III. Jesus concludes with his judgment of the two prayers (v. 14).

Homiletical outline
I.   The problem with religion is that it is based on figuring out how good we are.
   A.   We try to prove we are good by a negative index.

B. We show how good we are by a positive index.
C. We protest our goodness by comparing ourselves to those who appear sinful.

II. To receive God's mercy requires that we admit we can't make it alone, regardless of how religious we might be.
A. To understand our need of God, we begin by distancing ourselves from attempts at being seen as good.
B. God's forgiveness comes not just when we feel sorry for our sins.
C. To be judged forgiven requires sacrifice.

III. God's upside-down kingdom requires that to be affirmed to others we must act with humility.

The big idea

We don't need to be good to be forgiven, but we need to be honest about ourselves and repentant.

Not only is the Pharisee not better off than the tax collector, he is worse off because the tax collector at least had the sense to realize his enormous need. What one knows and the other does not is that they both are dead and in need of resurrection (Capon 1988, 181).

Material in order of the text

> ⁹To some who were confident of their own righteousness and looked down on everybody else, Jesus told this parable:

The parable begins with Luke's observation that Jesus is telling this parable to those who "were confident of their own righteousness and looked down on everyone else."

As we listen to this story some two thousand years later, layered with a negative view of the Pharisees and because we know the story's outcome, it is important that in the sermon we listen as the crowd did and condition ourselves to expect what *should* happen, rather than what we know did happen. Our prejudice against the Pharisees is so complete that it is helpful to point out that Pharisees were not all hypocritical and super-legalistic but played a vital role in the life of the people, even as the historian Josephus saw them as people known for their good deeds and love for the Torah, the Book of God.

> [10]"Two men went up to the temple to pray, one a Pharisee and the other a tax collector."

As much as we today are conditioned to see the Pharisee as the one who will be rejected, it really is the tax collector we should expect Jesus to condemn.

Even though the tax collector was considered low on the moral scale of the Jewish citizenry, as a Jew he would have every right to enter the court of the Israelites. If he was unclean as defined by Jewish law, there were cleansing facilities in the temple area.

Coming into the temple during sacrifice—in the afternoon—these two men would stay for prayers and then return to their homes (Bailey, *Through Peasant Eyes*, 146).

> [11]"The Pharisee stood up and prayed about himself: 'God, I thank you that I am not like other men—robbers, evildoers, adulterers—or even like this tax collector.'"

There is nothing in this that signals to the listening Jews that there is anything wrong with this story. Those standing in the temple would be more like the Pharisee than the tax collector and for him to thank God for his life was a good thing. He begins with giving God thanks for everything; his goodness is based on God. His prayer of gratitude that he is not like others would produce envy in those listening for they would want to congratulate him on his good living. He was a good man: Three things he mentions—thievery (he does not swindle), doing evil (he is not hypocritical), sexual impurity (he is not unfaithful).

The phrase "he prayed about himself" either can be interpreted as a kind of a soliloquy in which he is speaking to himself about himself or could mean that he was speaking to God (note Hultgren, 118). It seems, however, that the Pharisee, in praying "about himself," was likely speaking to God because later the tax collector, as he speaks about himself, is speaking to God. As the Pharisee speaks of his accomplishments, the tax collector speaks about his failure.

The Pharisee deliberately sets himself in contradistinction to the tax collector ("or even like this tax collector"). The term "even like" (*e kai hos*) adds to the Pharisee's "condemnation of sin to the denunciator of a sinner" (Herzog, 186).

Just as the high priest enters to burn the incense for the prayers—
a moment the people wait for—the Pharisee speaks up and makes
his goodness known. Note the body language: The Pharisee "stood
up," in contrast to the tax collector.

> [12]"'I fast twice a week and give a tenth of all I get.'"

The Pharisee moves from telling God what he doesn't do to telling
God what he does do. This makes him remarkable.

Because he was able to fast twice a week (Monday and Thursday),
it suggests he was sufficiently well-off to allow him this discipline.
In addition to the Day of Atonement, Yom Kippur (Lev. 16:29-31;
23:27, 29, 32; Num. 29:7), and other special days, the Pharisee rou-
tinely fasts twice a week, which increases the public's admiration of
him. Those listening in the temple would be impressed with that.

For the Pharisee to tithe everything he owned or ate meant that
he was careful to live a pure and undefiled life. So not only was he
highly disciplined, he went the extra mile to ensure his purity. As a
pious man, he was admired.

The Pharisee, in bringing the temple tax, not only was acknowledging his gratitude to God but also was ensuring that next year's crops
would be large. If one did not bring the temple tax it would result
in two problems: First, one would be considered unclean because
of eating produce that had not been tithed; and second, it put one
further in debt to God, a debt that built from year to year with no
possibility of ever getting out from under the oppressive load.

These demands on the people served the priests and their families
as they lived off of the temple tax. The priests who lived in Jerusalem profited from a "second tax" that served to enhance the priestly
families who lived there. Over time, however, this system resulted in
increased impoverishment of the poor and increased riches for the
wealthy (Herzog, 179).

> [13]"But the tax collector stood at a distance. He would not even
> look up to heaven, but beat his breast and said, 'God, have mercy
> on me, a sinner.'"

The Pharisee is a foil for the tax collector. Standing a good distance
from the Pharisee, on the margin of the temple, the tax collector is
ostracized by the elite and condemned by those watching. He is so

ashamed that Jesus observes he cannot lift his eyes. The Greek *ouk éthelen* suggests a personal choice not to look up (Jones, 245).

This tax collector is different from Zacchaeus (Luke 19:2), who, as a chief tax collector, could give away half of his goods because of the amount of capital he handled and the size of his personal wealth. This tax collector could not do that. He was a small player and probably could not repay what he had taken because it had already been spent.

Note that though the tax collector says little, much is said about his posture, contrasting with the Pharisee, of whom little is noted of his posture and much of what he said.

The Tax Collector's Stance. We expect that, after hearing the Pharisee, the tax collector will silently slip away, outmatched by the performance of the one so admired by others as being holy. One might even feel sorry for him. Here he is, possibly standing by the eastern gate, put down and outclassed by the righteous one. But, to our surprise, he does not remain silent after he hears the "holier-than-thou" prayer of the Pharisee. The labels, understood by those gathered for prayers, make it clear that the tax collector is one of those who is undermining the religious life of the people of God.

Instead of competing with the Pharisee or appealing to the crowd for understanding, the tax collector goes to a higher source. He peels off the label. In the overpowering silence following the speech of the Pharisee, he slaps his chest and breaks the silence with a mournful phrase, simple and unimpressive. Rejecting the idea that the judgment of the Pharisee is the same as the judgment of Yahweh, he makes his own plea. While most of those listening would think it is the best plea he can make, they would agree that his ability to gain God's notice was limited.

He looks to the altar where the priest has offered a sacrifice for the people. He sees the blood dripping into the gutter. In effect, he says, "Lord, I see the sacrifice that has been made for the sins of the people. Please accept that sacrifice for me." He is not asking God to be kind to him because he is different from the Pharisee. He directly accesses what is rightfully his: atonement. He has come to realize that anything good he could do would not be enough. The only possibility of acceptance he has is to take advantage of what the Lord had provided in the atonement.

The Tax Collector's Words. He cries out, "God, have mercy on me, a sinner," at the hour of sacrifice and by so doing invokes the language of sacrifice. Onlookers agreed with his need to call out for the sacrifice, for note what kind of sinner he is seen to be:

a.   He has defrauded his people.
b.   He associated with the Gentiles in this evil scheme of toll gathering.
c.   It would be interpreted that he has robbed the temple of its due taxes by forcing people to pay taxes rather than tithes.
d.   By so doing he is complicit in forcing his people into a life of impurity because their tithe was not paid.
e.   He ends up supporting the Roman occupation rather than the Jewish system.

The irony is that he asks for atonement for his sins in the very place he has helped desecrate by way of his toll gathering.

His plea for mercy is accompanied by a striking of the chest, the heart or source of his sin. Rather than listing his sins—as the Pharisee had listed his accomplishments—the toll collector cries out at the time of atonement, "Oh God! Let it be for me! Make an atonement for me, a sinner!" (Bailey, *Through Peasant Eyes*, 154).

The phrase he uses, "have mercy on me," is better translated "make atonement for me" (McBride, 190). The only other time this verb (*hilasthèti*) is used is in Hebrews, "that he might make atonement for the sins of the people" (2:17). In other places, where the noun *hilastèrion* is used, it is always rendered "atonement" and not "mercy" (Rom. 3:25; Heb. 9:5; 1 John 2:2; 4:10). It makes sense that the tax collector speaks of atonement and not mercy, for his request is at the time of sacrifice; he speaks out of his immediate context.

> [14]"I tell you that this man, rather than the other, went home justified before God. For everyone who exalts himself will be humbled, and he who humbles himself will be exalted."

This is the only time the word *justified* is used for an individual in the Gospels. In other places it is used only within a court setting. This is, in effect, a court in session as in a "trial by prayer" (Donahue 1988, 190). The Judge decides: The prayer of the tax collector is accepted, the prayer of the Pharisee is not. The trial ends as Jesus pronounces the verdict; the tax collector is exalted and the Pharisee humiliated.

The tax collector shows, in contrast to the Pharisee, that fasting is not what God requires but rather mourning and repentance, very much in the tradition of the Hebrew prophets (note Isa. 58:3-9).

The listening Jews are speechless! They do not need an explanation as to why this despised clod has been forgiven. What they need is to be consoled. Their expectations have been reversed. Their assumptions have come toppling down. They thought they had it figured out and now they are caught by surprise. Their entire worldview is turned on its ear. Their world has gone crazy. The very temple that rose out of God's instructions in early centuries seems to be shattered into fruitless religious exercise.

Jesus "reverses normal standards of divine approval and how this approval is experienced. The Pharisee is a moral person who in fasting and tithing even goes beyond legal requirements. Yet, as with the older brother [of The Prodigal Son], his God exacts dutiful service, which isolates him from others. The tax collector simply asks forgiveness. The justice of God accepts the unjust and the ungodly and judges the virtuous. The paradox of the kingdom is supported by the paradox of the two protagonists" (Donahue 1988, 190).

Homiletical considerations

1. The challenge in preaching this parable to postmoderns is to overcome the popular view of Pharisees as only being hypocrites. Because of this, it is important that the Pharisee in this parable be reintroduced as he would have been seen in Jesus' day. The importance of the Pharisee in parables for the church leader of today—be it the pastor, elder, prayer warrior, Christian education teacher—is that our pride, explicit or implicit, is rejected by God, who turns to the humble and community scoundrels who trust only in his mercy.

2. In taking time in the early part of the sermon to address this, it will lead people to get inside the story and then feel the shock those listening to Jesus would have felt when the tax gatherer is singled out as being the one who receives mercy.

3. Underlying this parable is Jesus' judgment that religious pride is an affront to him. Note that he tells this "to some who were confident of their own righteousness and looked down on everybody else."

4. Jesus here is rejoicing in the very worst who reach out in humility for his forgiveness.

5. Again, the challenge in preaching a parable is to provide sufficient information about the setting and story without the sermon becoming just a retelling of the story. The preacher can drop in interesting points that explain what is going on and add qualitative information about the parable. The sermon is not a retelling of the story but a linkage to satisfy the question, What does this look like on Monday morning on the factory floor or in the business office?

6. There are four major movements in the parable:

- a. By giving emphasis to the place the temple plays in the life of the Hebrew community, the setting of prayer holds up the temple's significance in the life of the people of faith.
- b. The Pharisee is central and needs appropriate describing so the linkage to a comparable contemporary group is made.
- c. The tax collector also needs to be described so the congregation understands whom he might represent in today's world.
- d. Jesus' conclusion is a perfect opportunity to explain that to be affirmed as good we must act with humility, otherwise the opposite of what we hope for will occur.

Conclusion

These ten parables, as part of the some twenty-seven recorded in the Gospels, sufficiently indicate the opportunities parables provide in preaching to postmoderns. While parables do not cater to postmodernity's overall vision, they do provide a window through which the gospel can be communicated. For a preacher, the challenge is not to allow the message to become subservient to the culture, yet at the same time to recognize that parables uniquely open the way into postmodern thought. While stories appeal to all generations and cultures, that is not the only reason why Jesus' parables are helpful in appealing to a postmodern culture. In preaching parables, it is important for preachers to understand a postmodern worldview and to appeal to that as an opening device in achieving the purpose of the sermon and the call of the gospel of Jesus Christ.

Unique preaching windows to postmoderns these parables provide

The Sower: Matthew 13:1-23. A rather simple story of farming that provides an opportunity to appeal to their interest in creating a place in which the kingdom seed will have a hospitable space in which to grow.

The Unforgiving Servant: Matthew 18:21-35. Ethics as an issue of vital concern, bridges into Jesus' call for a transformation of the "heart."

Laborers in the Vineyard: Matthew 20:1-16. Human rights and fairness are at the heart of postmodernity, which becomes a premise from which Jesus makes his appeal for his followers to trust in God's fairness.

Talents: Matthew 25:14-30. Since postmodernity is more a creation of the more prosperous developed world, those preaching in places of less abundant wealth will need to find ways in which "talents" connect to their world. In either case, the challenge is to make it clear of one's ultimate accountability to God.

The Good Samaritan: Luke 10:25-37. Pluralism as the operative paradigm of a postmodern culture is the window this parable opens, and by so doing provides a test on how much we love God with how much we love our neighbor.

The Friend at Midnight: Luke 11:1-13. Prayer and spirituality are part of the postmodern vision of holism. Jesus doesn't let it rest in neutral. Instead, he calls those who trust him to fan the flame of faith.

The Rich Fool: Luke 12:13-34. Aging as a condition of the baby boom generation provides a window through which the outcomes of life are inevitably measured.

The Prodigal Son: Luke 15:1-32. This parable's story of human failure and forgiveness can be followed up with an appeal to believe in the story of God the Father, who in Christ humiliated himself to prevent the ultimate humiliation.

The Persistent Widow: Luke 18:1-8. While justice is a byword of postmodernity, the surprise is the widow's pursuit of justice, which is a call for people to press God for justice.

The Pharisee and the Tax Collector: Luke 18:9-14. The rejection of religious absolutes, so central to postmodern thought, links naturally to a rejection of the Pharisee. The challenge is to lead from this to Jesus' message of humility as the way to forgiveness.

4

Four Sermons

1. The Unforgiving Servant (Matthew 18:21-35)
2. Talents (Matthew 25:14-30)
3. The Good Samaritan (Luke 10:25-37)
4. The Prodigal Son (Luke 15:11-32)

THESE SERMONS ARE BUILT ON THE FOUNDATION of the preceding material: location of the text within the wider biblical context, special word analysis, cultural issues, verse-by-verse analysis, homiletical outlines, and preaching considerations.

These sermons have been written with the assumption that few notes will be used in the actual preaching of the sermon.

Sermon One: The Unforgiving Servant

Text (Matthew 18:21-35)

> [21]Then Peter came to Jesus and asked, "Lord, how many times shall I forgive my brother when he sins against me? Up to seven times?"
>
> [22]Jesus answered, "I tell you, not seven times, but seventy-seven times.
>
> [23]"Therefore, the kingdom of heaven is like a king who wanted to settle accounts with his servants. [24]As he began the settlement, a man who owed him ten thousand talents was brought to him. [25]Since he was not able to pay, the master ordered that he and his wife and his children and all that he had be sold to repay the debt.

[26]"The servant fell on his knees before him. 'Be patient with me,' he begged, 'and I will pay back everything.' [27]The servant's master took pity on him, canceled the debt and let him go.

[28]"But when that servant went out, he found one of his fellow servants who owed him a hundred denarii. He grabbed him and began to choke him. 'Pay back what you owe me!' he demanded.

[29]"His fellow servant fell to his knees and begged him, 'Be patient with me, and I will pay you back.'

[30]"But he refused. Instead, he went off and had the man thrown into prison until he could pay the debt. [31]When the other servants saw what had happened, they were greatly distressed and went and told their master everything that had happened.

[32]"Then the master called the servant in. 'You wicked servant,' he said, 'I canceled all that debt of yours because you begged me to. [33]Shouldn't you have had mercy on your fellow servant just as I had on you?' [34]In anger his master turned him over to the jailers to be tortured, until he should pay back all he owed.

[35]"This is how my heavenly Father will treat each of you unless you forgive your brother from your heart."

Title

"Arthur Andersen and God: Both Have Odd Accounting Systems"

The big idea

The benefits of forgiving someone who owes me $15,000 are enormous, for God then forgives me the $9 billion I owe God.

Purpose

To help the audience understand that as we expect God to forgive us our sins God expects us to forgive as well, and then to lead the audience to forgive someone who has wronged them, and to do it before next Sunday. (See chapter 3, pp. 44ff.)

~

Jeff Nordick, after completing his MBA, got the job of his dreams working for the Pacific National Bank. Within eighteen months he was made department manager and within two years chief of investment banking. The market was on a roll: It seemed nothing he did went wrong. He bought the BMW of his dreams. He and his wife found a most romantic home in Rosedale—an upscale community in the city. And to make sure his friends had a place to party on summer weekends, he bought an expensive log cottage in a resort area, just two hours north of the city.

Wanting to cash in on the rising tech stocks, he used his position at the bank to leverage a major loan to invest in what he believed was a sure bet. The people running the start-up company were buddies of his from university, bright minds that he knew could make not just millions but possibly billions of dollars for the investors.

Everything was going fine, until a Wall Street firm sent a notice to investors to sell tech stocks. Within weeks the NASDAQ had dropped by half, and Jeff's investment, which had been soaring at $75 a share, plummeted to a penny stock.

If Jeff had invested his own money, he would simply have lost his investment. The problem was that he had invested borrowed money. It wasn't long before the bank president was asking him how he was going to repay the loan. Jeff knew it was impossible. Even if he sold his Rosedale home and the log cottage, he'd have nowhere near enough to pay back what he owed.

As he sat across the table from the president, he could feel the sweat trickle down his back. He remembered Bernard Shaw's line, "Forgiveness is a beggar's refuge. We must pay our debts." Jeff was known for being a smart negotiator, a guy who could talk his way through tough deals. This time, however, he knew he was cornered. Not willing to admit defeat, he looked at the president and bluffed, "Mr. Surrey, just give me an extra eighteen months and I'll have this loan repaid."

Jeff watched his president, looking for signs he had been persuasive again. The president looked out across the city from his fifty-seventh-story window, then slowly turned back and said, "Jeff, I know what has happened to the tech stocks and the financial hit you've suffered. Because of the great work you do here at the bank I'm going to exercise the discretionary powers the board of directors has given me and write off this loan."

Jeff couldn't believe his ears: Over $3 million forgiven! His darling BMW was still his, he and his wife wouldn't have to experience the humiliation of moving from their prestigious home, and now he wouldn't have to drum up some excuse to explain to their friends why the cottage was no longer available.

It was time for lunch. Catching the elevator down to the concourse, he ran into Bill Elliott, a bank employee who worked on the trading desk. Bill and his wife, who were renting a house that Jeff owned as an investment, had also lost on the market and were behind in paying their rent.

Turning to Bill, Jeff asked him when the rent would be paid. Bill looked at him helplessly and said, "Jeff, I've run into some problems with this market downturn. Could you give me a few months to turn this around?"

Without a second's hesitation Jeff bluntly responded, "No way, Bill. You get that check to me tonight or you're out by month's end." And sure enough, on the thirtieth of the month Bill, his wife, and their three children moved in with her parents.

It didn't take long for this news to get back to the president. Calling Jeff in, George Surrey said angrily, "Jeff, you're nothing but a scoundrel. I went out of my way to keep you out of bankruptcy, forgiving more than I've ever done before. Then what did you do? You threw Bill and his family out of their house because he was three months behind in his rent. I'm going to do the same thing to you. I've just instructed the credit department to put a lien on your car, house, and cottage, and as of now you are fired. Now get out!"

~

As much time as Jesus spent with the disciples, they still didn't understand what he had come to do. They were preoccupied with ridding their country of outside powers and setting up what they truly believed would be David's kingdom.

To help them understand what his kingdom is, Jesus calls over a child. Pointing to the little one, he says that unless they become like a child they will never understand why he has come. He follows this with a parable of a loving shepherd who looks for one lost sheep and then follows it up with this parable on how they are to treat their debtors.

The real trigger to this parable is Peter's question: "Lord, how many times shall I forgive my brother when he sins against me? Up to seven times?" Rather than giving a direct answer, Jesus tells a story. As with all his parables, Jesus expects those listening—and therefore us—to figure out what he means.

The story begins with a man who doesn't show gratitude for the king's gift of forgiveness. Eventually, his blockheaded insensitivity robs him of the enormous blessing his king offers, and in the end his stupidity causes his downfall—not unlike how we often don't treasure the goodness that comes to us every day.

The other day our daughter called, as she does every evening after dinner. She is expecting her first child. Earlier she had had a life-threatening ectopic pregnancy, and we didn't know if she would ever be able to have children. How blessed we are to be part of the excitement of our daughter and her husband as they await the birth of this child.

For the past thirty-four years, God has allowed me to work with some of the finest people in ministry. We've planned great international events, and we've worked on local projects in which we've seen amazing answers to prayer.

I was raised in a minister's home and from an early age wanted to be a preacher, quite unlike my next-older brother, who wanted to be a medical doctor. The two of us have had the privilege of being asked to serve as leaders in our respective fields, doing things beyond our youthful imagination. Again, how blessed I've been to find fulfillment in my calling.

In all of this, however, there's a real danger that small issues will make me oblivious to the enormous blessings in life. Likewise, the manager in this parable makes no effort to keep on good terms with his generous king.

The king is reviewing his accounts receivable. He discovers that one of his managers owes him an enormous amount of money. The amount is so staggering that it seems beyond reason. And that's what Jesus intends. He uses hyperbole, or exaggeration, for effect. In today's currency, this servant would have owed the king some $9 billion! In effect, Jesus is saying, "Peter, you want to know how often we are to forgive? Let me tell you that because God has forgiven you an amount way beyond what you can imagine, the least you can do is forgive someone who owes you a few shekels."

We live in an age and society that play off the notion that getting through the pearly gates is really about balancing off our good against our bad, not unlike the karma of some Eastern religions. We assume that if we do enough good in life, we'll have a positive balance in heaven's ledger. Then, when we meet St. Peter, he'll see we've got more "brownie points" than sins and let us into heaven.

What this fallacious view does is make our failures seem like minor errors of judgment. Of course, we "know" that for really bad guys like Hitler and child molesters there is no chance they will ever see the light of heaven.

What does it mean to be in debt to God? What do we owe that is so massive that we have no hope of being able to pay it back? How could we pay off $9 billion? We can't, which is Jesus' point. He leaves it to us to conclude how we—who have been forgiven of such debt—should forgive those who owe us comparatively less.

Most of us are guilty of trivializing sin: We see our failures as nothing worse than poor judgment at best and a character flaw at worst. We excuse our "little sins" as being of small consequence. We end up not understanding the enormous debt we've accumulated, a debt we can never repay.

Some weeks after the terrorist strikes on the United States, a Canadian editor wrote that he had been duped into believing that evil was a figment of the imagination. Now he admitted he was wrong: Evil does exist.

Most of us recognize that evil exists. But for those of us who don't kill others, who don't fool around on our spouses, who don't cheat on our taxes, and don't beat our children, do we actually make the leap of logic and say that we too are evil? The Bible says we are every bit as guilty before God with our "little" sins as those are who do the really "big" stuff.

When we stand before God, we won't be measured by the size of our sins; we will be judged by whether or not the debt of our sin has been paid. That's the story of Jesus. He is the king who paid, not just part, but all of our $9 billion debt.

But how is that done?

Imagine going to the bank, knowing that your house, your car— indeed, everything you own—will be repossessed by a bankruptcy court because you can't pay your debt. Then, to your surprise, the bank manager walks around the desk to where you are standing, puts his arm around your shoulders, and says, "Hey, lighten up, your debt no longer exists."

That's what Jesus does. The enormous debt we've piled up by our many sins and by the sinful nature we've been born with have been cleared off the books, never to be remembered again. That is a strange accounting of our sins, but God's accounting plan—thankfully—is different from ours.

John writes, "If we confess our sins, he is faithful and just and will forgive us our sins and purify us from all unrighteousness."

However, suppose that just as you walk out of the bank you meet someone to whom you lent twenty dollars last week. Like you, I can't imagine that, just having been forgiven of my enormous debt, I'd walk up to the person, grab him by the scruff of the neck, and say, "Hey, you deadbeat. Hand over the twenty bucks you borrowed." What I hope I would do is to take the person out for coffee and during our conversation say, "Hey, the twenty last week—forget it."

You and I know that is what we should do on the money side. But what do we do with those with whom we've had opportunity to forgive other "debts" and haven't? After I've had my devotions, after I've spent time in the morning reading the Word of God, giving thanks for God's willingness to forgive me of attitudes, thoughts, and behaviors that are out of line with God's call, do I ever then refuse to forgive someone who has done me real wrong? It depends. If it is a petty grievance, I'm likely to write it off. But if it is much larger, it might be harder to forgive.

In the early history of the Jews, God makes a covenant with Moses. That is, God will keep God's side of the bargain if they will keep theirs. Our relation to God is a two-way street. God's heart for forgiving is enormous. Jesus came into life so that by his death and resurrection we would be forgiven of the unbelievable debt of our sin. We ask him to forgive and he does. Ask him this morning and again tonight and he will forgive again. But it doesn't end there. There is a covenant that is implicit when we ask him to forgive us, which is that we too are to forgive.

John, in a letter to Christians in the first century, writes:

> My dear children, I write this to you so that you will not sin. But if anybody does sin, we have one who speaks to the Father in our defense—Jesus Christ, the Righteous One. He is the atoning sacrifice for our sins, and not only for ours but also for the sins of the whole world.
>
> We know that we have come to know him if we obey his commands. The man who says, "I know him," but does not do what he commands is a liar, and the truth is not in him. But if anyone obeys his word, God's love is truly made complete in him. This is how we know we are in him: Whoever claims to live in him must walk as Jesus did. (1 John 2:1-6)

What keeps us from forgiving? What holds us back from giving to others what has been given to us?

First, it is hard to admit the narrowness of our world; we're reluctant to admit that we are more like the manager than the master. Every day, living in the greatness of God's creation, breathing the air, eating the produce, living in relationships that give us pleasure, we assume they are ours by right. In enjoying these opportunities, it seldom strikes us that we are enormously in debt to God.

As well, we are trapped in our own small worlds, believing that we are the only ones not being treated fairly. Welfare recipients are angry because they aren't getting more money. Executives of mining and pulp companies complain they aren't given easier access to natural resources. Union worker Jimmy Hoffa, when once asked what his union wanted, famously replied, "More." Am not I among these? Too often ungrateful for the unending rewards, not of my labors but of others', I end up wanting more while at the same time missing opportunities of blessing others.

Why is forgiveness so essential to living the kingdom of Jesus? What is there in forgiving others that is so liberating?

Forgiving someone forces me to understand that the other person may, in fact, not be aware of the offense. As Jesus is being crucified, he cries out, "Father, forgive, for they don't know what they are doing." The Romans and Jewish leaders do not know that they are killing the Son of God.

Forgiving also releases us to receive God's gifts. By forgiving others, we deny evil a stronghold in our lives. By forgiving others as God forgives us, we keep our hearts and lives in tight relation with God.

At Jesus' crucifixion, on either side of him are two thieves. One verbally assaults Jesus, demanding that he help them, while the other asks for forgiveness. The second thief, in admitting his own failure, recognizes Jesus as the one unfairly convicted. What happens to this thief? Jesus promises him that on that very day he will be in heaven. The thief's request opens him to receiving all that God has for him.

While the manager in Jesus' parable has everything to gain fiscally by being kind to the one who owes him money, Jesus wants us to know that there is a reciprocal action in forgiving. We don't forgive only so he will forgive us, but in forgiving we are replicating what God has done for us and by so doing we open our lives to the wealth and richness of God's kingdom. It begins, as I recall, with

God's forgiveness of $9 billion. The benefits of forgiving someone who owes me $15,000 are enormous, for God then forgives me the $9 billion I owe him.

I enjoy some of the stories of the East. One such story is of a peasant walking along the road one day; he sees a billboard displaying an invitation to all the citizens of the kingdom to come to the king's palace for a great feast. The peasant reacts with a bitter expletive. "How dare the king invite us all?" he mutters. "He knows many of us can't come in the rags we wear." The more he thinks about it, the angrier he becomes.

Finally, he walks to the palace and pounds on the gate, demanding to see the king, but the guard pushes him away. Day after day the peasant demands to see the king. Finally, the king hears about this strange request and instructs his guards to let the peasant in the next time he comes to the gate.

One day, to the peasant's surprise, the gate opens and he is escorted into the king's throne room. All of a sudden he isn't so bold. The king, looking up from his work and seeing the peasant, says, "My subject, please rise and give me your request."

The peasant rises, no longer feeling courage. "I-i-s i-i-t true," the peasant stutters, "that we are all invited to your palace for a feast?"

"Why, of course," the king replies.

The peasant looks down at his rags, wondering how he could tell the king of his embarrassment. The king (so the story goes) is a kind sort and, understanding the peasant's plight, calls for his son.

The son takes the man into his apartment and, opening a panel, shows him an array of robes. "Help yourself," he invites.

The peasant, being self-conscious, doesn't move. So the prince picks out a magnificent purple velvet robe and says, "Try it on."

The peasant drops his rags and pulls on the garment. He has never felt such luxury. Embarrassed, he stoops to tie up his rags and, clutching them in his hand, mutters his word of thanks and slips home.

The day of celebration comes. The king has a great time watching his many citizens. He notices the peasant looking regal in the purple robe. Music is being played, and food is being passed down the long tables. The king turns again to see the peasant, but as he does his heart sinks. Moving to get a better look as to the reason for the problem, he knows there is nothing he can do.

The problem is this: The peasant is holding in his left hand the bag of rags and he doesn't have a free hand to dish the food to his own plate as the guests pass the platters of food along the table. For the entire feast he takes no food.

Weeks later the king hears that the peasant friend is dying. He goes to the peasant's hut; he stoops through the low door and there, lying on a bamboo mat, is his friend, still dressed in his regal purple velvet robe, now somewhat smudged and torn. The king lifts the peasant, now just skin and bones, but still clutching the bundle of rags.

The story concludes with the king speaking softly, "My dear friend, if you'd only let go of your rags, all the food on my tables was yours."

When I hold on to an unforgiving spirit, I'm the one short-changed. Drop the rags of your unforgiving spirit and go out of your way this week to forgive someone who owes you something. If you need to speak to the person, do it carefully and in a gentle and humble way.

Next week, drop me a note and tell me what happened. The benefits of forgiving someone who owes you $15,000 are enormous, for God then forgives you the $9 billion you owe God.

Sermon Two: Talents

Text (Matthew 25:14-30)

[14]"Again, it will be like a man going on a journey, who called his servants and entrusted his property to them. [15]To one he gave five talents of money, to another two talents, and to another one talent, each according to his ability. Then he went on his journey. [16]The man who had received the five talents went at once and put his money to work and gained five more. [17]So also, the one with the two talents gained two more. [18]But the man who had received the one talent went off, dug a hole in the ground and hid his master's money.

[19]"After a long time the master of those servants returned and settled accounts with them. [20]The man who had received the five talents brought the other five. 'Master,' he said, 'you entrusted me with five talents. See, I have gained five more.'

[21]"His master replied, 'Well done, good and faithful servant! You have been faithful with a few things; I will put you in charge of many things. Come and share your master's happiness!'

[22]"The man with the two talents also came. 'Master,' he said, 'you entrusted me with two talents; see, I have gained two more.'

[23]"His master replied, 'Well done, good and faithful servant! You have been faithful with a few things; I will put you in charge of many things. Come and share your master's happiness!'

[24]"Then the man who had received the one talent came. 'Master,' he said, 'I knew that you are a hard man, harvesting where you have not sown and gathering where you have not scattered seed. [25]So I was afraid and went out and hid your talent in the ground. See, here is what belongs to you.'

[26]"His master replied, 'You wicked, lazy servant! So you knew that I harvest where I have not sown and gather where I have not scattered seed? [27]Well then, you should have put my money on deposit with the bankers, so that when I returned I would have received it back with interest.

[28]"'Take the talent from him and give it to the one who has the ten talents. [29]For everyone who has will be given more, and he will have an abundance. Whoever does not have, even what he has will be taken from him. [30]And throw that worthless servant outside, into the darkness, where there will be weeping and gnashing of teeth.'"

Title
"Use It or Lose It!"

The big idea
Use it or lose it.

Purpose
To help the audience know we are held accountable for the gifts, skills, and opportunities given to us by God. (See chapter 3, pp. 66ff.)

~

If I asked you to help me list the most deadly sins, what would you include? Most of us would begin with those noted in the Ten Commandments and then add a few more. But how many of us would include failing to use the potential God has given each of us?

That is why this parable is so surprising: not that we doubt that God cares how we handle what has been given us, but that it matters so much. Why is Jesus so harsh on the one who hides his investment money? Do you hear the judgment of Jesus?

> Take the talent from him and give it to the one who has the ten talents. For everyone who has will be given more, and he will have an abundance. Whoever does not have, even what he has will be taken from him. And throw that worthless servant outside, into the darkness, where there will be weeping and gnashing of teeth. (vv. 28-30)

My goodness, this servant doesn't give the money away as a bribe, he doesn't use it for a good time, he doesn't even use it to pay off his mortgage. Instead, he simply protects it until the king returns. And what does he get for what seems a rather modest error of judgment? "Throw that worthless servant outside, into the darkness, where there will be weeping and gnashing of teeth."

But why? Why does he invoke such a ferocious outburst? Does it mean we will go to hell if we don't invest what God has given us?

Before we run off and start a new church that teaches that we get into heaven by our good works, let's carefully examine the text to see what Jesus is saying.

Throughout the Bible there is an underlying understanding that God sees what we do. After Jesus' resurrection, he ascends back to the Father with the promise that he will return. Though we have been given much, we are warned not to take it for granted. Just as at work we are evaluated, so God evaluates us today and every day and on that final judgment day.

This idea of accountability that Jesus presents to his disciples is not new. Note that this story is not for the religious leaders or crowds but for his disciples—those who live with him every day. Jesus wants these ones to hear how tough and demanding God really is.

If you are a Christian, one who believes that Jesus is the Son of God, and if you trust in his death and resurrection as the payment for your sin, then this story is for you. For when we come to Christ in faith, a new life is born in us. One of the results of that new life is that someday we will live forever with Jesus.

But there is another aspect to being a follower of Jesus: We now understand that our Creator invests in us God's life, by the gift of the Father's Son and by God's Spirit who lives in us. We now have a responsibility to live out God's life in the world.

You may not see yourself as a Billy Graham or a Mother Teresa, but that doesn't mean that in God's eyes you aren't as important. Of the three levels of investment in this parable, you may not see yourself as the five-talent or even the two-talent person. Regardless, to each of us God gives something of value to be used for God.

There is a danger that when we think about accountability we believe that we will face it only in the future. We reason this way: Because Jesus' return is in the future, my time of accountability will only be then. Not so. Here is the paradox: While it is true that Jesus is returning to earth in the future, he is already here. So, being judged or being held accountable is something that is going on all the time. Jesus holds me accountable for the use I make of his gifting today: It isn't only a matter of some future time, it is happening every day. God keeps short accounts.

An important question you may ask is, "What has God placed in me that matters so much to God?" If I'm going to be judged on how I've used these talents, wouldn't it be helpful to know what God is talking about? Here is a sampling of what some of these "gifts" may be:

1. The very fact that I'm a human being is remarkable. In Genesis we learn that God's imprint is upon us. The term *imago Dei* means that we are a divine imprint. The God of creation fashioned us to resemble the divine essence. We aren't a cheap reproduction, stamped out in God's cosmic factory. We humans are a divinely designed gift in this world.

2. Lily and I are fascinated by our grandchildren, born to the same parents and yet so different. I'm from a family of five children and each of us has different personalities. What a statement of our Creator: We are unique, unlike any other. Each of us has something to contribute to this world.

3. As we are different by way of personality, we are also different by way of talents. The imagery is that God has deposited gifts that differentiate each of us, gifts that have potential for good in God's world.

4. The older I get, the more I realize that one of the most important "commodities" of my life is time. Because of the busyness and pace of life, it's easier to send a check off to help a mission than to give of my time.

5.   Within my personality and gifts, there are opportunities that
     come to me and no one else. What am I to do with these? Are
     they not a gift that requires a choice, a risk in taking the oppor-
     tunity or doing nothing?
6.   Have you noticed how we tend to have two kinds of relation-
     ships: those few that hold together over the years and those that
     vary with time, place, vocation, and interests? God has uniquely
     gifted me with both longtime and short-term friends who have
     made a difference in my life. Our investment in each other reaps
     enormous dividends.
7.   Paul describes other gifts that God invests in our lives: the spe-
     cial gifts of the Spirit. Here is what he says:

> Now to each one the manifestation of the Spirit is given for the
> common good. To one there is given through the Spirit the mes-
> sage of wisdom, to another the message of knowledge by means
> of the same Spirit, to another faith by the same Spirit, to another
> gifts of healing by that one Spirit, to another miraculous pow-
> ers, to another prophecy, to another distinguishing between spir-
> its, to another speaking in different kinds of tongues, and to still
> another the interpretation of tongues. All these are the work of
> one and the same Spirit, and he gives them to each one, just as he
> determines. (1 Cor. 12:7-11)

Some years ago I visited a maximum-security prison on the East
Coast. The chaplain of the prison wanted me to meet Lillian, an
extraordinary grandmother.

Her story begins soon after her husband died. One Sunday after
church, during a missions conference, she went home wondering
what she could do at her age: Her children were gone, her husband was
now dead, and she was alone, operating a small insurance agency.

Monday morning, her pastor called. "Lillian, a woman is coming
from the west to visit her son in prison, and she has nowhere to stay.
Could she stay with you?"

Lillian was delighted. Living alone in her large house, she loved to
have people stay with her.

The woman arrived and after a few weeks of visiting her son in
prison it was time to return home. "Lillian," she said, "there is no
one to visit my boy. Would you mind driving out there occasionally
and visit him?" Lillian agreed and some days later drove the twenty-
five miles to this most imposing, ancient, castlelike structure.

She walked through the gates, past the metal detector, and across the visiting room to meet her recent friend's son. She told me, "Brian, as I approached this young man, I heard a voice saying, 'Woman, behold your son.' From that moment I loved him."

Over the next months, Lillian visited the young man often. His inmates, noticing this grandmother with her hugs and cookies, asked if she would visit them too. Soon her life was taken up with loving more and more inmates of this maximum-security prison, reserved for society's most dangerous offenders.

An official in the penitentiary system later told me, "We noticed after Lillian had started visiting that the level of violence seemed less. We also noticed that guards began taking inmates out to their homes. It is one thing when inmates become religious, but it's something more when guards show this kind of interest."

What was unique about Lillian? One doesn't usually associate being a grandmother with helping prisoners. But Lillian was exactly what God needed. She was old enough that the sordid business of men in prison and their sexual needs was not an issue. She knew they needed love and needed God. God's gifts in her life paid huge dividends because she was willing to invest them in the lives of others. She knew well that if one doesn't use one's gifts they are lost.

The tough issue in this parable is to figure out what Jesus is saying to the third servant, who buries his money. Why these harsh and damning words: "Throw that worthless servant outside, into the darkness, where there will be weeping and gnashing of teeth"?

Let's start by looking at what Jesus does not mean.

First, he is not saying that if our investment fails we'll be thrown into a place of damnation. His words, "Throw that worthless servant outside, into the darkness, where there will be weeping and gnashing of teeth," are a way of saying, "Get the heck out of here."

Second, Jesus is not saying that how we manage our gifts is to be equated with acceptance into his kingdom. Such entrance is based on his love for us, not on our good works. While I don't want to soft-sell his message, we must not confuse his reminder that we will be held accountable with our getting into heaven.

Jesus is not speaking here to the unconverted; he is speaking to his disciples. This "tough love" message is for those who follow him, those who are willing to leave all to serve him. It's a message he wants his followers to hear.

Finally, the consequence of our actions is not just what happens after we die. Yes, we will stand before his throne in eternity and be called on to give account for what we have done. But Jesus holds us accountable today and every day. The implications of what I do today are judged today. This accounting is not held in abeyance until the far-off future.

Having noted what Jesus did not mean, what then is he saying? The king begins by congratulating his people on their good work. In today's currency, the equivalent amount the king entrusts to the first servant is close to $2 million. When the king returns from his travels and sees this servant has increased the capital, he is excited and puts him in charge of a large enterprise, saying, "Come and share your master's happiness."

He then looks at the second servant, who also doubled his investment, and gives the same congratulations. Both people, though given different amounts, are congratulated. What did they do?

We don't know if one has more experience with investments or is better educated. All we know is that they are given a significant amount of cash and told to invest it. They take a risk, make good investments, and, by so doing, are rewarded.

The third servant is unwilling to take a risk and hides the money. When asked why, he simply says he was afraid. Then he offers an excuse that is an accusation against his king. He defends his actions by reminding the king that he knows his boss takes from places he has not invested, and so he hides the money. This argument is weak, having no connection to his veiled accusation.

Even if the king did as the servant accuses him of doing, why would knowing that lead the servant to bury the money? It makes no sense unless the servant is trying to detract from his own failure.

The king doesn't defend or excuse himself. He just says that if that is true, then the least the servant should have done was to deposit the money and add interest to the principal.

The severity of the king's judgment alerts us to an important message. What is it that Jesus sees as being so wrong? Why do we forfeit opportunities to risk investing our gifts?

This parable challenges the play-it-safe mentality. We are pulled up short by a cautious and lackadaisical attitude that seeks to preserve respectability or excuses us because of age. The danger with the church's being led by baby boomers is that our reflex becomes more and more for self-protection, to make sure that in the last few years of ministry "we end well." While it is good to live out our final years of ministry in faithful, Christ-honoring service, the danger is that our vision is determined by our ability to achieve and our goals are written to ensure success.

We also begin to operate out of fear and not faith. There is always the danger of failure. Investing in a project, a stock, an invention, or service does not mean one is guaranteed success. However, the nature of faith is to risk, not to be cautious. In God's upside-down economy, failure is due not to one's being prudent but to an unwillingness to take a risk. The Scriptures tell of those who risked in faith. What if Abraham had been careful to leave the lands of his parents in response to God's call or if Moses had been reluctant to lead the people of God into the promised land? Remember Peter, "If it is you, Lord, ask me to come on the water." Jesus replies, "Come," and Peter steps out of the boat.

When we hide a talent in the ground, it's like putting faith in a drawer for safekeeping. We take it out Sunday morning and display our symbol of faith in sacramental liturgy for an hour or so, maybe even adding some polish. Then, before afternoon football or golf, we put it back in the drawer as if it has nothing to do with how we live the rest of the week. To such behavior Jesus says, "Get out of my sight!" and gives the buried talent to the risk taker.

Listen to what the servant says in response to the king: "Yes, sir, I give back to you what was given. It's all here: 100 percent. Not a cent is missing. You see I know you, sir. I know that you grab anything in sight. You take from crops in which you didn't invest one seed. You are not only smart, you are tough. Knowing this, I said to myself, 'Self, walk carefully. Keep track of every red cent he's given you.' So I did what any careful accountant would do, I made sure every cent was in place when you returned. I didn't take one *mina* for myself. See, it's all here."

The master responds: "If you knew I was so tough, then why in the world did you protect your hind end? If there is one thing about me you should have known, it is that I don't let today be tomorrow. We don't live our lives protecting what we have. Instead, we look for opportunities today.

"Look, Abdul, when I invited you into partnership with me I knew your track record on investments. I trusted you. I gave you money to invest because I knew you had the ability to make good on it. I wasn't saying you *had* to make more, I was asking you to *try* and make more. I know there are no guarantees with investing. There is always the risk of failure. But no risk, no success. You either use it or lose it. I was asking you to take a risk, and you let me down. You played it safe. And by playing it safe, you not only didn't increase the $600,000 I gave you to invest, but you lost it. I'm taking it away and giving it to someone who has already demonstrated a willingness to take a risk.

"So get out of here, Abdul! I don't want you anywhere in sight. It's a dark world out there. No longer will you have the security of this household. See now if you can make it on your own."

There is an awful consequence for those who "bury" the opportunities of faith. But why does it matter so much? What is there about Jesus' kingdom that calls us to risk-taking? The Scriptures—from the very beginning with Cain and Abel and their offering to God, through to those who in the Revelation live by faith—make it clear that faith is essential to Jesus' kingdom.

The antithesis of faith is unfaith, like an "un-cola." We have a choice: to live in faith, believing that God has both called us and equipped us for God's service, or to live without faith, outside Christ's kingdom.

The focused message of this parable is that faith will be examined in judgment, which leaves us with the question: Are we willing to trust in the potential of God's gifts, even to the point of risk?

This risking in faith is not a function of one's personality type. One need not be a "type A personality" to be a risk taker. Neither is it the same as investing in the stock market or going out on a limb. Rather, it is trusting in the Holy Spirit to empower us in opportunities that come our way every day.

Faith can become entrenched in doctrine, sacramental form, styles of worship, and creeds, trapping us into a play-it-safe mind-set.

"Unfaith"—or the cautious side of faith—may arise from a need to be respectable. Radical faith is associated with those on the cultural fringe. But as such groups move up the socioeconomic ladder, they downplay their strengths to gain respect and acceptance. Church history is replete with stories of groups that have gone this route and have fallen into the trap of failing to use their gifts of faith. And, by not using their unique gifts, they have lost their dynamic witness.

In a very real sense, God needs us. To a critic who told Stradivarius—the great violin maker—that if God really wanted violins he could have made them himself, Stradivarius responded, "No, not even God could make my violins without Stradivarius." In a sense he was right. It's not that God "can't," for there is nothing God cannot do. But God created us humans to be God's comanagers—God chooses to have great violins made by great violin makers.

Each of us is given opportunities, and it is up to us to take advantage of them. The first two servants—one with five talents and the other with two—set off to make good in the opportunities given. In this story, each doubles his capital. Keep in mind this is a story and the amounts are symbolic. Nevertheless, the point is that each day there are opportunities to advance the kingdom. To see an opportunity as an investment helps us decide how to respond.

We either use it or lose it.

Take an inventory of your gifts. Keep it simple. Then ask, "Lord, what is there you've given me that I'm hiding?" You may even want to ask this question of others; get those who know and love you best to help you identify your gifts.

Then develop a dialogue with the Lord. Some find it helpful to keep a diary so they can better see their thoughts a few weeks later. Identify one or two "gifts"—and by that I mean abilities, opportunities, time, financial resources—and begin to plan ways they might be used. Finally, bathe the process in prayer. Don't allow past failures to determine how much you are willing to risk. Focus on Christ's call and the possibilities your investment may bring.

Believe that as God calls, God equips. Joshua, as he stands by the river asking God how they can cross into the promised land, is told that as the feet of the priests touch the water, the waters will part. The sea won't separate before faith is exercised. When he obeys, God holds back the water.

As you use it, your faith will grow. How much better than losing it.

Sermon Three: The Good Samaritan

Text (Luke 10:25-37)

[25]On one occasion an expert in the law stood up to test Jesus. "Teacher," he asked, "what must I do to inherit eternal life?"

[26]"What is written in the Law?" he replied. "How do you read it?"

[27]He answered: "'Love the Lord your God with all your heart and with all your soul and with all your strength and with all your mind' ; and, 'Love your neighbor as yourself.'"

[28]"You have answered correctly," Jesus replied. "Do this and you will live."

[29]But he wanted to justify himself, so he asked Jesus, "And who is my neighbor?"

[30]In reply Jesus said: "A man was going down from Jerusalem to Jericho, when he fell into the hands of robbers. They stripped him of his clothes, beat him and went away, leaving him half dead. [31]A priest happened to be going down the same road, and when he saw the man, he passed by on the other side. [32]So too, a Levite, when he came to the place and saw him, passed by on the other side. [33]But a Samaritan, as he traveled, came where the man was; and when he saw him, he took pity on him. [34]He went to him and bandaged his wounds, pouring on oil and wine. Then he put the man on his own donkey, took him to an inn and took care of him. [35]The next day he took out two silver coins and gave them to the innkeeper. 'Look after him,' he said, 'and when I return, I will reimburse you for any extra expense you may have.'

[36]"Which of these three do you think was a neighbor to the man who fell into the hands of robbers?"

[37]The expert in the law replied, "The one who had mercy on him."

Jesus told him, "Go and do likewise."

Title
"It's Not Rocket Science"

The big idea
In loving my neighbor whom I can see, I learn to love God, whom I can't see. And in loving God whom I can't see, I learn to love my neighbor whom I can see.

Purpose
To help the audience understand that loving God is tied to loving their neighbor and to lead them into discovering God's love by loving a neighbor this week. (See chapter 3, pp. 75ff.)

~

Let me tell you a story.

A Christian radio station invited three students from a Christian college to perform an on-air reading of the well-known biblical story of the Good Samaritan. As the students walked into the studio they were met by a smelly, unkempt man who asked if they would help him. One said he was late for a radio program; the young lady, obviously fearful, mumbled something; and the third turned his head as if he hadn't heard. None stopped to help. Little did they know that they had been set up. The "vagrant" was part of a scheme to test them.

If you've wondered about your responsibility when you see a World Vision special or walk out of a restaurant and are confronted by a street person asking for money, then you are in good company. Each of us is forced to ask, Who and what is a neighbor? This question asked of Jesus so many years ago is as current as today's newspaper.

Let me make a suggestion: Since you have heard this parable before, there is the danger that you may assume there is nothing further for you to learn from it. I suggest that we take a few moments to read it again. As I read, why not close your eyes and ask the question, "What is there in this story that I have not thought of before?"

> On one occasion an expert in the law stood up to test Jesus. "Teacher," he asked, "what must I do to inherit eternal life?"
>
> "What is written in the Law?" he replied. "How do you read it?"
>
> He answered: "'Love the Lord your God with all your heart and with all your soul and with all your strength and with all your mind'; and, 'Love your neighbor as yourself.'"
>
> "You have answered correctly," Jesus replied. "Do this and you will live."
>
> But he wanted to justify himself, so he asked Jesus, "And who is my neighbor?"
>
> In reply Jesus said: "A man was going down from Jerusalem to Jericho, when he fell into the hands of robbers. They stripped him of his clothes, beat him and went away, leaving him half dead. A priest happened to be going down the same road, and when he saw the man, he passed by on the other side. So too, a Levite, when he came to the place and saw him, passed by on the other

side. But a Samaritan, as he traveled, came where the man was; and when he saw him, he took pity on him. He went to him and bandaged his wounds, pouring on oil and wine. Then he put the man on his own donkey, took him to an inn and took care of him. The next day he took out two silver coins and gave them to the innkeeper. 'Look after him,' he said, 'and when I return, I will reimburse you for any extra expense you may have.'

"Which of these three do you think was a neighbor to the man who fell into the hands of robbers?"

The expert in the law replied, "The one who had mercy on him."

Jesus told him, "Go and do likewise."

All my life I've loved God. I can't remember a moment when I didn't want to serve him. As a boy, I loved church summer camp: There I could listen to three sermons a day. I learned Bible stories. I memorized Scripture. I went to church activities. If you had asked me what I was going to be in life, the answer would have been "a preacher."

I know something about being religious. And I know a lot of people who profess their love for God and their desire to serve God. The question before us is not, Is it important to love God? We already know that. What we want to know is, What does loving God look like?

The lawyer in this parable is most religious. His whole life has been spent in learning the Hebrew law. Not unlike a professor of theology at a seminary, this man is smart and knows the shades of the debate. His entire life is given to understanding God and helping the people to understand and obey God. This is not an unbeliever or heretic. He is a religious blue blood.

I suspect, however, that he had no real interest in finding a definition for "neighbor." What we know is that in this discussion he is testing Jesus, whom he likely has met before. It is a small community and, with one being an expert in the Law and the other a teacher of the Law, they probably know each other. When the lawyer asks Jesus his question, he is testing Jesus' orthodoxy. As an expert in Hebrew law and rabbinical commentaries, he is concerned about what Jesus is saying around Israel.

His opening question sets off a verbal tussle: They are like two heavyweights, testing each other in a public match. The lawyer begins by asking how he can obtain eternal life but ends up learning the test for loving God.

When Jesus responds to the lawyer's question with, "What does the Law say?" they are off and running.

Note the lawyer's response: "Love the Lord your God with all your heart and with all your soul and with all your strength and with all your mind" and "Love your neighbor as yourself."

What is curious about his response is that you won't find this quote anywhere in the Old Testament. Instead, it is a combination of two verses:

> Hear, O Israel: The LORD our God, the LORD is one. Love the LORD your God with all your heart and with all your soul and with all your strength." (Deut. 6:5)

And,

> Do not seek revenge or bear a grudge against one of your people, but love your neighbor as yourself. I am the LORD." (Lev. 19:18)

So why does the lawyer bring these two verses together? Teachers of the Hebrew law—like preachers today—link together verses from various parts of the Scripture. This is what he did in answering Jesus' question. He may have heard Jesus do this before, or possibly it was something he had heard in a message from another rabbi.

In any case, he gives Jesus the right answer, to which Jesus responds with a nod, "Do this and you will live. You asked your question, now you have your answer."

The lawyer has two choices: walk away or push the debate in a new direction. He chooses the second. He won't go in the direction about loving God for, after all, he assumes he knows all he needs to know about that; he is a professional religious person. He is orthodox and leads an honorable life. He obviously loves God; otherwise, why was he giving his life to knowing and living out the Law?

Like him, I measure my love for God with a self-testing kit: How often do I go to church? Do I pay the tithe? Do I cheat on my income tax? Do I read girly magazines? It is not unlike a student who raises a hand in class and asks, "Professor, do we have to learn this for the exam?" When I know how much I have to do or what the rules are, then I can assess whether or not I've made the grade. The more religious we become, the more we want to measure ourselves and others.

The lawyer's interest is not in knowing *how* to love but *who* to love. He wants to limit his exposure. He may assume that Jesus will say, "Why of course, your family and friends," and the lawyer will smile, say "Thanks," and walk away with the affirmation that he is good and therefore will gain eternal life.

Do you see the big movements in this story? Luke starts us off with the debate that Jesus has with this bright lawyer who asks how one inherits eternal life. This swings to the matter of loving both God and neighbor. To the seeming innocent question, "Who is my neighbor?" we are treated to one of the great stories of all time.

We, however, want to get past our twenty-first-century lens and try to see it as those did who were privileged to hear these two heavyweights in verbal debate.

The setting for the story is a lonely seventeen-mile stretch of road from Jerusalem at 2,500 feet above sea level to Jericho at 770 feet below sea level. Just before Jesus was born, Herod had let go forty thousand workmen. So there are plenty of unemployed people around now making a living as thieves. This road is feared by everyone: It is like walking alone at night through a gang-turf or a drug-infested neighborhood.

We don't know the victim—but he is probably a Jewish businessman. There are two ways to identify a person. One way is by language, and many spoke more than one of the many languages of that region, including classical Hebrew, contemporary Hebrew, Mishnaic, Greek, Samaritan, Latin, Phoenician, and Aramaic.

You can also identify a person by his or her clothing. In fact, you can even tell if someone is from your village by his or her manner of dress. The problem is, this man is unconscious and stripped naked. There is no way of telling who he is.

The first person along is a priest on his way from Jerusalem, where he serves in the temple. Up to ten thousand priests and Levites, many of whom lived in Jericho, went up to Jerusalem to serve for a week at a time. The priests were of the upper class in Jewish society.

The priest comes along and sees the person along the side of the road. When he looks down and sees the man stripped and unconscious, he has no idea who he is.

If the man isn't a Jew, it creates a problem, for a Jew would not want to touch a non-Jew. And if he is dead, then the priest will be defiled, which creates an even greater problem. In Jewish law, if you come within four cubits or six feet of a dead person you are considered unclean. But you need to get closer than that if you are going to see if the man is dead!

Priests collected and distributed the tithe brought to the Jerusalem temple. If the priest touches this man, especially if he is dead, then the priest will be defiled, unable either to take the food at the temple or to distribute it to his family or servants. He will have to go through a full week of cleansing, and then suffer humiliation by having to stand at the Eastern Gate with the defiled. In the end, he will lose four weeks' pay. So he is trapped!

Those listening to the story would have exclaimed, "Hey, the priest was smart for bypassing the robbed man. Anyone with a reasonable brain would know he had to look after himself, his family, and his servants first!"

Then, along comes the Levite, the lowest of the three orders in Israel's priesthood. It is his job to assist the temple priests on Sabbaths and feast days.

He, like the priest ahead of him, is bound by the same laws of uncleanness as the priest. Furthermore, he is afraid of robbers. When he arrives at the scene, he knows the priest has gone on, so how can he, a lesser person in the religious pecking order, do what the priest refused to do? he asks himself. And with no donkey, how can he really help?

Those listening to this story assume there are three types of people in the story: priests, Levites, and laymen. They would expect the third person to be a Jewish layman, but here the sequence is disrupted. The drama takes a sharp turn. The hero should be a Jewish peasant, but instead it's a Samaritan.

Who are the Samaritans, and why are they hated so much? Samaritans are Jewish half brothers from the north, born out of mixed Jewish and Philistine blood. Being part Jew, they are bound by the Torah and the Law, as are the priest and the Levite. But they are also heretics. A few years earlier, some Samaritans scattered human bones in the temple court. It is like Hindus desecrating a Sikh temple in the Punjab. Here the hated Samaritan becomes the hero, and that is the shock. It's like making a member of the PLO the hero of an Israeli play.

The Samaritan also faces the problem of contamination. As well, he is a prime target for robbers: Thieves might respect the priest or the Levite, but who cares about Samaritans? The priest and the Levite have ignored the man in trouble, and he may ask himself, "Why should I help?"

Overriding matters of vulnerability or religious distinction, Jesus describes the man's gut-level reaction: He "took pity" on the victim. He feels deeply this poor man's need. Although he is in Jewish-dominated territory, the need requires action. Cerebral concerns and rationalizations are out. Higher issues are at stake. The instinct of helping one in need is a God instinct. We mirror God when our lives reflect God's imprint.

Then notice what the Samaritan does: He uses wine to disinfect the wounds and oil as salve to aid the healing process. And where else are these elements used? In the temple. They are used in worship back up in Jerusalem.

Not only does Jesus throw in a surprise by the person who helps, but this one, so despised, is the only one who connects temple worship to everyday life. What we do in worship on Sunday is not removed from the situations we meet the rest of the week. As oil and wine are used to worship God in the temple, so are they to be used to disinfect and heal.

The priest and the Levite, as professionals, used oil and wine in their temple worship. In fact, they have just finished their work in Jerusalem. But when human need stares them in the face, it never occurs to them that what they use for worship can also be used for healing. Instead, it is the hated Samaritan who gives the ultimate worship, and by obedience uses temple material for good.

I take this story personally, for I'm not unlike the priest and the Levite. The Levites were given no land when they arrived in the promised land, as their only task was to serve the religious life of the people. They were, in the best sense of the word, professionals. I, too, am a church professional. I've given my life to serve the church, and, in turn, I'm supported so that my full life is given in this service.

I also go to church and pray to the God who hears me; I ask God to meet my needs; I expect the forgiveness God has promised. I absorb God's Word and confess to Christ's death and resurrection, especially around the communion table. The oil and wine of my life are God's grace—God gives me what I don't deserve—and God's mercy—God doesn't give me what I do deserve. These I carry with me, as it were, from the temple in Jerusalem to Jericho, from worship on Sunday to living the faith on Monday.

The big question is, While I carry these with me, do they stop with my professional service or are they used to heal and mend someone who is bleeding and broken?

If loving God, whom I can't see, involves loving a neighbor whom I can see, what does it cost to see? What is the cost in being a neighbor? We know with God nothing is without cost. While God's grace is free, it obliges those who want to be called by God's name.

So, what does being a neighbor involve? Surely it is more than saying "hi" to Alice as we both leave our driveways in the early morning or helping Tom out if he needs assistance in building a toolshed in the backyard.

Look what it costs the Samaritan. It is inconvenient: He has to interrupt his schedule, and at the most inhospitable of places—in the middle of a desert. He is vulnerable: The area is infested with robbers, to whom he, when stopping, might become a likely prey. There is the possibility of retaliation, one of the most instinctive social and human realities that define life in the Middle East. Because there is no inn nearby, he takes the man with him into Jericho, where he runs the risk of meeting the man's family, who will hold him accountable for the loss of blood. He is like a Syrian or Libyan carrying a mutilated American soldier into a Jewish base in the Bekka Valley in southern Lebanon. And it hits his wallet. He makes no attempt to be anonymous: He tells the innkeeper he will return and pay if the cost is more. There is a personal price. The price is not just money. Like Jews, he too—by touching blood or a dead body—would be defiled under the law and required to go through the ritual cleansing: a time-consuming process, and, for a businessperson, that means income.

From the question of loving God and then an example of what it means to love God, Luke moves us forward to Jesus' final question: "Which of these three do you think was a neighbor to the man who fell into the hands of robbers?"

The answer is obvious. But what is not so obvious is that while we profess to love God we often miss the connection to loving our neighbor. It is that linking of the two commands that calls our attention: If we can't love our neighbor, how can we love God? For it is in loving our neighbor that we learn to love God.

Notice where Jesus sets the parable—between Jerusalem and Jericho. And what do they represent? Jerusalem is the center of worship, the holy place where people go to meet God. There the highest form of worship is experienced and expressed. Jericho is the city Joshua cursed when the children of Israel first broke into the promised land: "Cursed before the Lord is the man who undertakes to rebuild this city, Jericho" (Josh. 6:26).

Jesus connects these two cities and by doing so tells us that in his world there is no distinction between the divine and the profane, sacred and secular, holy and worldly: All is the Lord's. You can't worship in Jerusalem and then walk to Jericho as if what you have done in the temple has nothing to do with what you see on the road. God's call to us is to offer the wine of forgiveness and the oil of healing to those we meet.

In effect, in loving God whom we can't see, we'll be able to love our neighbor whom we can see. And in loving those we can see, we enter into loving God, whom we can't see.

As I begin each day, I do so with a prayer that my life will express the life of the Lord. I'm serious about it. I'm religious in that I believe that my relationship with God is the most important aspect of my life, today and forever. I want to love God. But then I move into my day, and without fail I meet someone I dislike, someone who bothers me, or someone who, if I help, will cause a delay or annoyance.

Here is the potential disconnect: If I fail to help, I'm denying that God cares for that person, for God's way of loving our neighbor is through those who say they love God. And if I who profess to love God do not show that love, then, as this story points out, I'm really saying that I haven't learned to love God, and then those in need whom I meet miss out on God's love.

And worse: As I continue to blind my eyes, deafen my ears, harden my heart, I drift away from loving God and I lose my ability to hear the divine voice, for God speaks through the neighbor he wants me to love.

Again, in loving God whom we can't see, we'll be able to love our neighbor whom we can see. And in loving those we can see, we enter into loving God, whom we can't see.

The galling part of the story to the religiously orthodox is that the one who is a theological deviant is the one who has learned to love God more.

I was invited by the late Barbara Frum, host of the Canadian television program *The Journal*, to participate in a public debate on AIDS. It was held in a downtown Toronto theater. As I walked in, I knew I wasn't among friends. When Barbara introduced me, there was a distinct "boo" from the crowd. This reaction shifted my opening line to, "It seems you judge me before I've had opportunity to speak, something you accuse us of doing." There was brief silence and then a polite applause, at which I felt a certain relief!

Sitting around the table were a number of medical and social-welfare professionals, including Al, a schoolteacher who was dying from AIDS. My assignment was to answer the religious questions, and while I knew my task was to try and speak biblical truth into the debate, I was not ready for what happened that night.

During the roundtable discussion, Al asked a question. As I turned to him, instead of seeing his failings, it was as if the Spirit used his eyes as a mirror and I saw myself. And what I saw was not attractive. I saw pride, hatred, revulsion, and self-righteousness. I struggled through the taping. I knew I had been found out. I had brought no humility to the discussion. Spiritual pride ruled. After the taping, I walked around the table, put my arms around Al and told him I loved him. It was my way of confessing my sin of pride and restoring a spirit of humility. Without that spirit, my works and words had become clashing cymbals.

Draw a straight line this week between your real love for God and the way you treat someone you meet who is in need. Loving God is no more complicated than that. Today and tomorrow or any day this week, ask who is your neighbor and what you do in that moment better describes how you love God than anything else. For in loving my neighbor whom I can see, I learn to love God, whom I can't see. And in loving God, whom I can't see, I learn to love my neighbor whom I can see.

Sermon Four: The Prodigal Son

Text (Luke 15:11-32)

[11]Jesus continued: "There was a man who had two sons. [12]The younger one said to his father, 'Father, give me my share of the estate.' So he divided his property between them.

[13]"Not long after that, the younger son got together all he had, set off for a distant country and there squandered his wealth in

wild living. [14]After he had spent everything, there was a severe famine in that whole country, and he began to be in need. [15]So he went and hired himself out to a citizen of that country, who sent him to his fields to feed pigs. [16]He longed to fill his stomach with the pods that the pigs were eating, but no one gave him anything.

[17]"When he came to his senses, he said, 'How many of my father's hired men have food to spare, and here I am starving to death! [18]I will set out and go back to my father and say to him: Father, I have sinned against heaven and against you. [19]I am no longer worthy to be called your son; make me like one of your hired men.' [20]So he got up and went to his father.

"But while he was still a long way off, his father saw him and was filled with compassion for him; he ran to his son, threw his arms around him and kissed him.

[21]"The son said to him, 'Father, I have sinned against heaven and against you. I am no longer worthy to be called your son.'"

[22]"But the father said to his servants, 'Quick! Bring the best robe and put it on him. Put a ring on his finger and sandals on his feet. [23]Bring the fattened calf and kill it. Let's have a feast and celebrate. [24]For this son of mine was dead and is alive again; he was lost and is found.' So they began to celebrate.

[25]"Meanwhile, the older son was in the field. When he came near the house, he heard music and dancing. [26]So he called one of the servants and asked him what was going on. [27]'Your brother has come,' he replied, 'and your father has killed the fattened calf because he has him back safe and sound.'

[28]"The older brother became angry and refused to go in. So his father went out and pleaded with him. [29]But he answered his father, 'Look! All these years I've been slaving for you and never disobeyed your orders. Yet you never gave me even a young goat so I could celebrate with my friends. [30]But when this son of yours who has squandered your property with prostitutes comes home, you kill the fattened calf for him!'

[31]"'My son,' the father said, 'you are always with me, and everything I have is yours. [32]But we had to celebrate and be glad, because this brother of yours was dead and is alive again; he was lost and is found.'"

Title

"From Pigs to Parties: The Saga of Love"

The big idea
Regardless of my foolish choices, God the Father looks for me to turn my steps homeward.

Purpose
To lead people into understanding how much God deeply loves each of us and to invite them to choose before they leave church to begin the journey homeward today. (See chapter 3, pp. 108ff.)

~

When Jesus tells his stories, he does so to real people. He isn't speaking "to those of you in radio-land." They are a real, flesh-and-blood audience. Luke tells us in chapter 15 that four kinds of people sat listening to this one.

There were tax collectors, Jews used by Rome that added an enormous burden on their fellow citizens. It's estimated that 40 percent of a person's income went to pay taxes. There were the "sinners," a collective term for people we go out of our way to avoid such as panhandlers or drug dealers. There were the Pharisees, a group whom I think get a rather bum rap today. About 150 years before Christ, as Palestine was being freed from outside armies, a movement that we now know as the Pharisees began to protect the Hebrew culture from being overrun by Greek culture, called Hellenism. It was something like the Canadian Radio and Television Commission in Canada today: This federal agency is doing all it can to keep Canada from being overrun by the cultural domination of American radio, TV, and the print. As well, in the listening crowd there were the scribes, or teachers of the Law, who, Luke tells us, were grumbling about Jesus' consorting with sinners. What a crowd!

To understand the power of this story, I'm going to try to fill in what those listening that day would have understood to be between the lines. So, let's take off our Walkman headphones of today's culture and listen to Jesus as if you and I were sitting there that day.

> Now the tax collectors and "sinners" were all gathering around to hear him. But the Pharisees and the teachers of the law muttered, "This man welcomes sinners and eats with them."...

Jesus continued: "There was a man who had two sons. The younger one said to his father, 'Father, give me my share of the estate.' So he divided his property between them.

"Not long after that, the younger son got together all he had, set off for a distant country and there squandered his wealth in wild living. After he had spent everything, there was a severe famine in that whole country, and he began to be in need. So he went and hired himself out to a citizen of that country, who sent him to his fields to feed pigs. He longed to fill his stomach with the pods that the pigs were eating, but no one gave him anything.

"When he came to his senses, he said, 'How many of my father's hired men have food to spare, and here I am starving to death! I will set out and go back to my father and say to him: Father, I have sinned against heaven and against you. I am no longer worthy to be called your son; make me like one of your hired men.' So he got up and went to his father.

"But while he was still a long way off, his father saw him and was filled with compassion for him; he ran to his son, threw his arms around him and kissed him.

"The son said to him, 'Father, I have sinned against heaven and against you. I am no longer worthy to be called your son.'

"But the father said to his servants, 'Quick! Bring the best robe and put it on him. Put a ring on his finger and sandals on his feet. Bring the fattened calf and kill it. Let's have a feast and celebrate. For this son of mine was dead and is alive again; he was lost and is found.' So they began to celebrate.

"Meanwhile, the older son was in the field. When he came near the house, he heard music and dancing. So he called one of the servants and asked him what was going on. 'Your brother has come,' he replied, 'and your father has killed the fattened calf because he has him back safe and sound.'

"The older brother became angry and refused to go in. So his father went out and pleaded with him. But he answered his father, 'Look! All these years I've been slaving for you and never disobeyed your orders. Yet you never gave me even a young goat so I could celebrate with my friends. But when this son of yours who has squandered your property with prostitutes comes home, you kill the fattened calf for him!'

"'My son,' the father said, 'you are always with me, and everything I have is yours. But we had to celebrate and be glad, because this brother of yours was dead and is alive again; he was lost and is found.'"

Most of us have stories of wanting to get out from under the rule of our parents. I so wanted to be off on my own that I left my family at our cottage by the lake, choosing to work on a farm. The farmer saw a good thing coming his way: a strong teenager who wouldn't know—at least at first—that he was being taken to the cleaners. I worked and worked and worked and got next to no pay: I soon learned that living at home wasn't so bad after all.

The young man in this story wants the same: to live his life on his own. He begins by putting before his father a request to receive his inheritance. In a patriarchal society, such a question is devastating, for one's inheritance comes only after the father dies. So, what he is really saying is, "Dad, I wish you would drop dead!" Kenneth Bailey, expert on Middle East culture, says that, in all of his readings of modern and ancient literature, he has never read anything that acts as a cultural bomb the way this story does.

We know what we expect the father will do: He'll backhand this impudent son and send him on his way. But he doesn't. "Oh yes," we say to ourselves, "the older brother will do the diplomatic peace shuttle between father and son and patch up this nasty family squabble."

Wrong again.

Wealth then, as it is today in the Middle East, is land. To our amazement, the father gives him his one-third, and the son takes what he has (the phrase "got together" in verse 13 is a banker's term), leaving for a "far-off" city, which, in Jewish literature, means the most despised of all places, a Gentile city. But, to carry his inheritance, he has to sell the land. The sequence of events may go something like this:

The younger son goes next door, knocks on the door of Mr. Abe Suschovitch. After the usual greetings, the young man says, "Mr. Suschovitch, I have some land to sell."

"And what land is that?" asks Mr. Suschovitch. The young man, afraid that he would be asked that question, presses on: "My inheritance, sir."

Mr. Suschovitch, agitated, says, "Your father has died! But how is it that no one told me of his death? Why didn't you come over and let me know? I would have attended the funeral."

"No, no," replies the son. "Father didn't die. You see, I've asked for my inheritance."

"You mean the land that Moses left Egypt to inherit, and the land Joshua led us across the Jordan to conquer, the land we've fought for all of our lives? You mean to say the land your parents and great-grandparents have given their very souls to nurture and develop—you are going to sell it? How much?"

A deal is finally struck, and the young man has his inheritance in cash.

Notice the devastating slide Jesus describes: The son violates the patriarchal family; he insults his father; he takes the most precious commodity of the Middle East—land—and sells it; he leaves the land of promise to seek his fortune with the very tribes the Jews fought against to build their land, faith, and culture. How much further can he sink? we wonder, as the story continues.

In the Gentile city—and by that we know Jesus means a place where Jews should not choose to go—he loses his money and is such a failure that, with the local famine, he ends up feeding pigs. (You know how popular a ham sandwich is at a kosher lunch!) He is as far from the faith, home, and land of his people as he can go.

Your story may not be as devastating or dramatic as his. And it may be that your life has been lived within the boundaries of what is expected of you. But most of us, at some point in life, at least in our hearts, "move out" and lose much of what we started out with. As a preacher's kid, I've always been a pretty good actor. I had to be—I played with the deacon's kids!

Religious people get good at camouflage: We don't want others to know our problems, so we put on an act. But the more we act, the more we actually waste away what we had in the early days as we learned to walk with the Lord.

The young man, humiliated, hungry, and alone, thinks about going back home. But he faces a very big problem: There is a custom that if a man loses his money to Gentiles or marries an immoral woman, the enactment of the *gesasah* will be his fate. The towns-people will gather around him, smash a large pot filled with burned corn and nuts, and deny him the right to live in their village. This rite is for having insulted his father and embarrassed his hometown and villagers. But the young man decides that his food is so bad and his conditions so deplorable that it's worth the risk. There seems to be no sense of contriteness or real sorrow for his actions. He's hungry and alone. He is still the despicable son we met at the opening of the story. Far from the kind of son I would ever want.

On his way he develops a story for his father. First, he will say he has blown it and is no longer worthy to be called a son. Then we wonder what he will ask of his father. The language he chooses is precise. He could ask to be made into a bondsman (*dulos*), but he rejects that. He could ask to be a slave (*paides*) or a house servant (*diakonos*), but he rejects that too. Instead, he will ask his father to hire his as a skilled laborer (*misthos*). As a skilled laborer, he will be allowed to earn his way back into the good graces of his father and thereby the family and the community.

You can often see people's reaction to a situation or story by their body language. I can see the tax collectors and sinners holding their heads in their hands, as one mutters, "Has Jesus ever got my number! He sure has figured me out."

But the Pharisees seem pleased. The Pharisees had been disturbed by Jesus' teaching, for they believe God loves one only when one obeys the laws, and it seems Jesus is agreeing with their teachings. One is heard to say, "Maybe we've been too hard on this rabbi from Nazareth. It may be that he understands the nature of true religion more than we've given him credit for."

Isn't this what we've come to believe too? Don't we really believe that God keeps score? So if I end up with more points for doing good than negative points for doing bad, then God will love me.

If you were to die today and stand before God and he asked, "On what basis should I allow you into my kingdom?" wouldn't you want to see the cosmic charts, run your finger down the list until you found your name, and then hope against hope that you ended up with more pluses than minuses? That's what this younger son believed.

The story continues.

Picture the father seeing his son. As a farmer, he doesn't live on his farm as many do in North America. Because of the danger of roving bandits, everyone lives together in a village inside a stone fence, with one gate.

It may be in the evening, when the father is sitting on the porch drinking his Starbucks coffee and eating a bagel, that he glances over the fence and sees someone coming in the distance. At first he doesn't pay much attention, but then he notices the way the man is walking: "No one walks like that except my youngest son," he mutters to himself. He watches and watches, and the closer the man gets to the village, the more sure he becomes that it really is his son: "My goodness, the kid needs a haircut!"

It is here the story turns. Listen closely and you can hear people in the crowd sucking wind on this shocking shift.

What the father does at first doesn't appear to be remarkable to us. As the father sees his son approach, he knows what might very well happen: If the townspeople get to his son first, they may hold the ceremony of the *gesasah*. The father must decide quickly if he is to get to his son before the townspeople.

How can he get there first? In verse 20, he runs. Look at verse 20. While that is not an issue for us today, recall what men wore then. They wore robes. Have you ever tried to run in a robe? You've got to lift the robe so you won't trip. But that presents a dilemma. Men were not to show their legs. Indeed, in the first century there was a major rabbinical debate over whether a man could lift his robe when walking through thorns. So, what does the father do?

We see the drama unfolding. Children playing in the streets are shocked to see this man of stature running by, holding up his robe, embarrassing himself, all for the purpose of reaching the gate before the townspeople. The father arrives, throws his arms around his son, and, before his son can get out his confession, before the townsfolk can dishonor him, the father calls for the best clothes and a party to celebrate the return of his son.

The father humiliates himself to keep his son from further pain. Though the son's leaving was his choice and the humiliation to his father was his doing, that doesn't matter to the father. When his son turns his steps homeward, the father reaches out, accepting him as a full member of the family, and throws a party. Though the father has lost his land and suffered public embarrassment, his simple response is to love his son.

What triggered this response? Did the son undo his sins? Did the son repay for the lost land? Did the son repair the humiliation his actions brought to his family and father? No. All he did was turn his steps homeward.

Regardless of my foolish choices, God the Father looks for me to turn my steps homeward.

Each of us at some time in our life squanders our inheritance—be it our reputation, family love, or our personal gifts—and wanders off. Some of us have done it with no one noticing. For you see, as religious people we know how to act, and our performances can be very convincing.

Philip Yancey, in his book *What's So Amazing about Grace?* tells the story of a teenager in Traverse City, Michigan, who thinks her parents are too old-fashioned. One day they react to her shorter skirts and ground her.

That's it for her. She isn't going to take it anymore, so she runs away from home, ending up in Detroit.

On her second day there she meets a man in a big, flashy car. He seems so nice. He takes her for a ride and then out to a fancy restaurant. Later that day he puts her up in a fancy hotel room and then suggests she might want to try some pills that will make her feel really good.

Two months pass, during which he teaches her what to do with men. Living in a penthouse, she forgets about her modest home in Traverse City. She once has a scare when she sees her picture on a milk carton with the caption, "Have you seen this child?"

A year passes and signs of illness begin to show. She notices that the man who was so nice to her begins to be mean. She has less and less money. She now finds she has to pay for her drugs. It gets worse and worse. Eventually, the man locks her out of the penthouse, and she is forced to find a place to sleep wherever she can keep warm. Now, feeling like a little girl, she is lost and alone, without money, food, or friends.

She begins to remember home and the fun she had with her golden retriever chasing a ball. "God, why did I leave?" she asks herself a hundred times a day. It isn't many days before she decides that more than anything else in life, she wants to go back home. She finds some quarters for the phone, and after three tries and finding no one at home, she leaves a message. "Dad, Mom, it's me. I was wondering if I might come home. I'm catching a bus up your way and I'll get there at midnight tomorrow. If I don't see you at the station, well, I guess I'll just stay on the bus until it hits Canada."

For seven hours she's alone on the bus, traveling from Detroit to Traverse City. "What if my parents didn't get my message?" she wonders. Mile after mile she practices her speech to her parents. At last the bus pulls into the station. The air brakes hiss and the driver shouts, "Fifteen minutes and then we move on. The next stop is Canada."

The frightened young lady looks in her compact mirror, licks off excess lipstick, and, knees knocking, walks into the terminal.

There, on plastic tables and chairs, stand forty of her brothers, sisters, aunts, uncles, cousins, and grandmother, all waving to her, wearing goofy hats and blowing noisemakers. Across the wall of the terminal they had taped a computer-printed banner. It reads, "Welcome home."

Her dad runs up to her and she has just enough time to blurt out two words: "Sorry, Dad. . . ."

"Hush, sweetheart. We've got a big party for you at home," he responds.

Regardless of my foolish choices, God the Father looks for me to turn my steps homeward.

Today is the day to turn your steps homeward. You may be at the point of despair: the condition of your life may be so complicated and disastrous that you wonder if there are any possible answers. There always are answers. The beginning is when you understand that, regardless of your foolish choices, God the Father looks for you to turn your steps homeward.

Or you may be on your way away from faith, determined to try it all. Would you listen to the life experience of this son and many who are here? Would you for a moment consider the enormous loss in living as if you mean nothing to God? You too can experience the surrounding love of God without throwing life away. It all begins by turning your steps home to the Father.

Notes

1. Postmodernity

1. Modernity—terms include *The Enlightenment* and *The Age of Reason*—refers to the modern era, beginning with René Descartes' maxim, up to the early 1970s. "This age of reason . . . embraced classicism with its order and rationality. . . . Reason alone, so they thought, may now replace the reliance on the supernatural born out of the ignorance of 'unenlightened times'" (Veith, 33).

2. "Postmodernism . . . holds that the so-called world that emerged intellectually from the sixteenth century onward has come to an end at the close of the twentieth century as surely as the so-called medieval era [premodern] early on had its day" (Carl F. H. Henry, "Postmodernism: The New Spectre?" in Dockery, 36).

3. "The Enlightenment project . . . took it as axiomatic that there was only one possible answer to any question. From this it followed that the world could be controlled and rationally ordered if we could only picture and represent it rightly. But this presumed that there existed a single correct mode of representation which, if we could uncover it . . . would provide the means to Enlightenment ends" (Harvey, 27).

4. "Descartes highlighted the rationalist standard of clear and distinct ideas, the sciences wielded empiricist criteria, the Hegelians placed their hope in Spirit's progress in history, and the Romantics appealed to an immediate pre-reflective intuition. These criteria provided a universal foundation for the disciplines" (Phillips and Okholm, 12).

5. Deists taught that, while God was necessary to get life started, it is not necessary that God have any continuing place in life (Veith, 34).

6. "Darwin's theory of evolution challenged romanticism just as it did Christianity. Darwin showed that nature was not the realm of harmony and goodness that the romantics idealized" (Veith, 37).

7. "Modern history is turning out to be embarrassing precisely on the basis of its own optimistic axioms. Not some theory but actual modern *history* is what is killing the ideology of modernity. I need only mention Auschwitz, Mylai, Solzhenitsyn's *Gulag Archipelago, Hustler* magazine. . . . All of these point to the depth of failure of the modern consciousness" (Oden, 51).

8. "Since all claims to truth are merely social constructions, truth is simply an honorific term used to describe our best guess at the way things are" (Steven Bouma-Prediger, "Yearning for Home," in Westphal, 172).

9. "Foucault's [an early voice of postmodern thought] connection between knowledge and power marks the postmodern end of the road that Francis Bacon charted at the beginning of the Enlightenment. . . . Human knowledge does not merely allow us to exercise power over nature . . . more significantly, knowledge is violence" (Grenz 1996, 133).

10. "Knowledge is no longer seen as absolute truth; rather, knowledge is seen in terms of rearranging information into new paradigms. Human beings *construct* models to account for their experiences. These models—whether worldviews or scientific theories—are 'texts,' constantly being revised" (Veith, 57).

2. Parables: A Window of Truth for Postmoderns

1. See Scott 1989, 63, 64; see Craig Evans, "Parables in Early Judaism," in Longenecker, 72–73.

2. Evans, "Parables," in Longenecker, 54.

3. Ibid., 56–61.

4. Ball, 97–111.

5. "Herdsman. A Keeper of domestic animals that go in herds. The word (Gn 13:7-8, 26-20; I Sm 21:7) is more often translated 'shepherd' (see Sheep)," *The Interpreters Dictionary of the Bible, E-J,* ed. George Buttrick et al. (Nashville: Abingdon, 1976), 2:221. "Interestingly, although the biblical shepherd was a cherished image of care for God's people, first-century shepherds were generally despised by the average Jew, due to their reputation for lawlessness and dishonesty (cf. b. Sanhedrin 25b)" (Blomberg, 180).

6. Note the Parable of the Good Samaritan: The teacher of the law quotes from the Old Testament (Luke 10:27).

3. A Study of Parables for Sermon Preparation

1. Some see no connection whatsoever between the two (Herzog, 132).

2. This amount is based on an example of a person earning a salary of $40,000 a year or $153 per day times 6,000, which equals $918,000. Mul-

tiply that times 10,000—the number of talents in the story—and the final amount is $9,180,000,000 (note Buttrick, 108; Donahue 1988, 63; Herzog, 143–44).

3. "The *Mishnah* contains a written collection of traditional laws handed down orally from teacher to student. It was compiled across a period of about 335 years, from 200 BC to AD 135," *Nelson's Illustrated Bible Dictionary* (Nashville: Thomas Nelson, 1986), 719.

4. "While Christians may see these teachings from the position of later faith, one is hard-pressed to attribute such theological implication to Jesus himself. Jesus is teaching about God's loving nature and challenging a response" (Young, 135).

5. "Primarily, originally and properly, the scribe and Pharisee does not reject merely a distasteful doctrine of sin and forgiveness, but the God who is the God of this man, the man who is the man of the God, the actuality of the Son of God and His humiliation, and of the Son of Man and His exaltation, the atonement which takes place in this One," Karl Barth, *Church Dogmatics*, trans. G. W. Bromiley, vol. 4, part 2 (Edinburgh: T. & T. Clark, 1936–62), 24.

6. "For Palestinian listeners, initially the father would naturally be a symbol of God. Then, as the story progresses, the father comes down out of the house and, in a dramatic act, demonstrates unexpected love publicly in humiliation. The literary structure and cultural milieu of the story identify this dramatic act as the turning point of the first half of the parable. Surely Jesus intended his listeners to see in this a dramatic representation of his welcome of sinners. When the father leaves the house to come out to his son in love and humility, he demonstrates at least a part of the meaning of the incarnation and the atonement" (Bailey, *Poet and Peasant*, 190).

7. "For it is not his remorse for the sins he has committed, but to begin with, quite simply the realization that he has come to the end of his tether, which makes the son turn back," Gunther Bornkamm, *Jesus of Nazareth* (New York: Harper, 1960), as quoted in Bailey, *Poet and Peasant*, 175.

8. Jeremias, in writing about the garment necessary for admission to the wedding feast, notes that "the white robe, or the garment of Life and Glory, is a symbol of the righteousness awarded by God (cf. esp. Isa. 61:10), and to be clothed with the garment is a symbol of membership of the redeemed community. It may be remembered that Jesus spoke of the Messianic Age as a new garment (Mk. 2:21) and that he compared forgiveness with the best robe with which the father clothed the prodigal son" (Jeremias 1972, 189).

9. The "how much more" technique in this parable works like this: "If this miserable judge eventually responds to the nagging of the widow and meets her request, *how much more* will our Heavenly Father meet us in our need?"

10. That the Pharisee said he paid a tenth to the temple indicated that he would have been faithful in paying the other taxes required by Rome and the Jewish laws. In effect, he is saying that there is no tax he avoids paying: His religious scruples are without question.

Bibliography

Allen, Diogenes. *Christian Belief in a Postmodern World: The Full Wealth of Conviction.* Louisville: Westminster John Knox, 1989.

Allen, Ronald J., Barbara Shires Blaisdell, and Scott Black Johnston. *Theology for Preaching: Authority, Truth and Knowledge of God in a Postmodern Ethos.* Nashville: Abingdon, 1997.

Anderson, Alter Truett. *Reality Isn't What It Used to Be: Theatrical Politics, Ready-to-Wear Religion, Global Myths, Primitive Chic, and Other Wonders of the Postmodern World.* San Francisco: HarperSanFrancisco, 1990.

Bailey, Kenneth E. *Parables.* Audiotapes of lectures given at an InterVarsity staff conference in Cyprus, ca. 1980.

————. *Poet and Peasant* and *Through Peasant Eyes: A Literary-Cultural Approach to the Parables in Luke.* Combined edition. Grand Rapids: Eerdmans, 1983.

Ball, Michael. *The Radical Stories of Jesus: Interpreting the Parables Today.* Regent's Study Guides 8. Oxford: Regent's Park College, 2000.

Barclay, William. *The Parables of Jesus.* Louisville: Westminster John Knox, 1999.

Bernstein, Richard J., ed. *Habermas and Modernity.* Studies in Contemporary German Social Thought. Oxford: Oxford University Press, 1985.

Blomberg, Craig L. *Interpreting the Parables.* Downers Grove, Ill.: InterVarsity, 1990.

Bloom, Allan. *The Closing of the American Mind.* New York: Simon & Schuster, 1987.

Boice, James Montgomery. *The Parables of Jesus.* Chicago: Moody, 1983.

Breech, James M. *Jesus and Postmodernism.* Minneapolis: Fortress Press, 1989.

————. *The Silence of Jesus: The Authentic Voice of the Historical Man.* Minneapolis: Fortress Press, 1983.

Brueggemann, Walter. *Texts under Negotiation: The Bible and Postmodern Imagination.* Minneapolis: Fortress Press, 1993.

Buttrick, David. *Speaking Parables: A Homiletic Guide.* Louisville: West-minster John Knox, 2000.

Capon, Robert Farrar. *The Parables of Grace.* Grand Rapids: Eerdmans, 1988.

———. *The Parables of Judgment.* Grand Rapids: Eerdmans, 1989.

———. *The Parables of the Kingdom.* Grand Rapids: Eerdmans, 1985.

Clements, Roy. *A Sting in the Tale.* Downers Grove, Ill.: InterVarsity, 1995.

Cook, David. *Blind Alley Beliefs.* Downers Grove, Ill: InterVarsity, 1996.

Corney, Peter. "Have You Got the Right Address? Post-Modernism and the Gospel." *Grid* (spring 1995): 1–7.

Coupland, Douglas. *Life after God.* Toronto: Pocket Books, 1994.

Crossan, John Dominic. *In Parables: The Challenge of the Historical Jesus.* Sonoma, Calif.: Polebridge, 1992.

Culbertson, Philip L. *A Word Fitly Spoken: Context, Transmission, and Adop-tion of the Parables of Jesus.* SUNY Series in Religious Studies. Albany: State University of New York Press, 1995.

Derrida, Jacques. *Positions.* Trans. Alan Bass. Chicago: University of Chi-cago Press, 1981.

———. *"Speech and Phenomena" and Other Essays on Husserl's Theory of Signs.* Trans. David B. Allison. Evanston, Ill.: Northwestern University Press, 1973.

———. *Writing and Difference.* Trans. Alan Bass. Chicago: University of Chicago Press, 1978.

Dockery, David S., ed. *The Challenge of Postmodernism: An Evangelical Engagement.* Grand Rapids: Baker, 1995.

Dodd, C. H. *The Parables of the Kingdom.* London: Fontana, 1967.

Donahue, John R. *The Gospel in Parable: Metaphor, Narrative, and Theol-ogy in the Synoptic Gospels.* Minneapolis: Fortress Press, 1988.

———. "Tax Collectors and Sinners: An Attempt at Identification." *Catho-lic Biblical Quarterly* 33 (1971): 39–61.

Drury, John. *The Parables in the Gospels.* New York: Crossroad, 1989.

Ford, Leighton. *The Power of Story: Rediscovering the Oldest, Most Natural Way to Reach People for Christ.* Colorado Springs: Navpress, 1994.

Ford, Richard Q. *The Parables of Jesus: Recovering the Art of Listening.* Min-neapolis: Fortress Press, 1997.

Fretheim, Terence E., and Karlfried Froehlich. *The Bible as Word of God in a Postmodern Age.* Hein-Fry Lectures. Minneapolis: Fortress Press, 1998.

Goetz, David. "The Riddle of Our Culture: What Is Postmodernism?" *Leadership* (winter 1997): 52–56.

Grenz, Stanley J. *A Primer on Postmodernism.* Grand Rapids: Eerdmans, 1996.

———. *Revisioning Evangelical Theology: A Fresh Agenda for the Twenty-First Century.* Downers Grove, Ill.: InterVarsity, 1993.

————. *Theology for the Community of God*. Carlisle, England: Paternoster, 1994.

Grenz, Stanley J., and John R. Franke. *Beyond Foundationalism: Shaping Theology in a Postmodern Context*. Louisville: Westminster John Knox, 2001.

Grey, Mary C. *Prophecy and Mysticism: The Heart of the Postmodern Church*. Edinburgh: T. & T. Clark, 1997.

Gunter, W. Stephen. *Resurrection Knowledge: Recovering the Gospel for a Postmodern Church*. Nashville: Abingdon, 1999.

Hanko, Herman C.. *The Mysteries of the Kingdom: An Exposition of the Parables*. Grand Rapids: Reformed Free Publishing Association, 1975.

Harvey, David. *The Condition of Postmodernity: An Enquiry into the Origins of Cultural Change*. Cambridge: MIT Press, 1987.

Hauerwas, Stanley. *After Christendom: How the Church Is to Behave if Freedom, Justice, and a Christian Nation Are Bad Ideas*. Nashville: Abingdon, 1991.

Hauerwas, Stanley, and David Burrell. "System to Story: An Alternative Pattern for Rationality in Ethics." In *Why Narrative?: Readings in Narrative Theology*, Stanley Hauerwas and L. Gregory Jones, eds. Eugene, Ore.: Wipf and Stock, 1997.

Heatherley, E. X. *The Parables of Christ*. Austin: Balcony, 1997.

Hedrick, Charles W. *Parables as Poetic Fictions: The Creative Voice of Jesus*. Peabody, Mass.: Hendrickson, 1994.

Herzog, William R., II. *Parables as Subversive Speech: Jesus as Pedagogue of the Oppressed*. Louisville: Westminster John Knox, 1994.

Hiebert, Paul G. *Missiological Implications of Epistemological Shifts: Affirming Truth in a Modern/Postmodern World*. Christian Mission and Modern Culture. Harrisburg, Pa.: Trinity Press International, 1999.

Hultgren, Arland J. *The Parables of Jesus: A Commentary*. The Bible in Its World. Grand Rapids: Eerdmans, 2000.

Hunter, Archibald M. *Interpreting the Parables*. London: SCM, 1960.

Iliffe, James. "Searching for Reality in a Postmodern Age." *On Being* (September 1996): 34–38.

Jeremias, Joachim. *The Parables of Jesus*. Upper Saddle River, N.J.: Prentice-Hall, 1972.

————. *Rediscovering the Parables*. London: SCM, 1966.

Jones, Peter Rhea. *Studying the Parables of Jesus*. Macon, Ga.: Smyth & Helwys, 1999.

Kalas, J. Ellsworth. *Parables of Jesus*. Nashville: Abingdon, 1997.

Keddie, Gordon J. *He Spoke in Parables*. Durham, England: Evangelical, 1994.

Keeney, William E. *Preaching the Parables: Series II, Cycle A*. Lima, Ohio: CSS, 1995.

————. *Preaching the Parables: Series II, Cycle B.* Lima, Ohio: CSS, 1996.

————. *Preaching the Parables: Series II, Cycle C.* Lima, Ohio: CSS, 1997.

Keller, Tim. "Preaching Morality in an Amoral Age." *Leadership* (winter 1996): 110–15.

Longenecker, Richard N., ed. *The Challenge of Jesus' Parables.* Grand Rapids: Eerdmans, 2000.

Lundin, Roger. *The Culture of Interpretation: Christian Faith and the Postmodern World.* Grand Rapids: Eerdmans, 1993.

Lyon, David. *Postmodernity.* Concepts in Social Thought. Minneapolis: University of Minnesota Press, 1994.

MacIntyre, Alasdair. *After Virtue: A Study in Moral Theory.* 2nd ed. Notre Dame, Ind.: University of Notre Dame Press, 1984.

Martin, Robinson. "Post What? Renewing Our Minds in a Post-Modern World." *On Being* 24/2 (March 1997): 28–32.

McBride, Denis. *The Parables of Jesus.* St. Louis: Liguori/Triumph, 1999.

McKenna, Megan. *Parables: The Arrows of God.* Maryknoll, N.Y.: Orbis, 1994.

McLaren, Brian D., *The Church on the Other Side.* Revised and expanded edition. Grand Rapids: Zondervan, 2000.

Meynell, Hugo A. *Postmodernism and the New Enlightenment.* Washington, D.C.: Catholic University of America Press, 1999.

Middleton, Richard J., and Brian J. Walsh. *Truth Is Stranger Than It Used to Be: Biblical Faith in a Postmodern Age.* Downers Grove, Ill.: InterVarsity, 1995.

Nelson's Illustrated Bible Dictionary. Herbert Lockyer Sr., gen. ed. Nashville: Thomas Nelson, 1986.

Newbigin, Lesslie. *Foolishness to the Greeks: The Gospel in Western Culture.* Grand Rapids: Eerdmans, 1986.

————. *The Gospel in a Pluralistic Society.* Grand Rapids: Eerdmans, 1989.

————. *Truth to Tell: The Gospel as Public Truth.* Grand Rapids: Eerdmans, 1991.

Nietzsche, Friedrich. *The Portable Nietzsche.* Ed. and trans. Walter Kaufmann. New York: Penguin, 1976.

Oden, Thomas C. *After Modernity—What?: Agenda for Theology.* Grand Rapids: Academie, 1990.

Oosterhoff, F. G. *Postmodernism: A Christian Appraisal.* Winnipeg: Premier, 1999.

Osborne, Grant R. *The Hermeneutical Spiral: A Comprehensive Introduction to Biblical Interpretation.* Downers Grove, Ill.: InterVarsity, 1991.

Osterley, W. O. E. *The Gospel Parables in the Light of Their Jewish Background.* London: SPCK, 1936.

Phillips, Timothy R., and Dennis L. Okholm, eds. *Christian Apologetics in the Postmodern World.* Downers Grove, Ill.: InterVarsity, 1995.

Postman, Neil. *Amusing Ourselves to Death: Public Discourse in the Age of Show Business.* New York: Penguin, 1985.

Reid, Barbara E. *Parables for Preachers: The Gospel of Mark, Year B.* Collegeville, Minn.: Liturgical, 1999.

Robinson, Haddon W. *Biblical Preaching: The Development and Delivery of Expository Messages.* Grand Rapids: Baker, 1980.

Roof, Wade Clark. *A Generation of Seekers: The Spiritual Journeys of the Baby Boom Generation.* San Francisco: HarperSanFrancisco, 1993.

Roxburgh, Alan J. *Reaching a New Generation: Strategies for Tomorrow's Church.* Downers Grove, Ill.: InterVarsity, 1993.

Scharlemann, Martin H. *Proclaiming the Parables.* St. Louis: Concordia, 1963.

Scott, Bernard Brandon, *Hear Then the Parable: A Commentary on the Parables of Jesus.* Minneapolis: Fortress Press, 1989.

————. *Jesus, Symbol-Maker for the Kingdom.* Philadelphia: Fortress Press, 1981.

Shillington, V. George, ed. *Jesus and His Parables: Interpreting the Parables of Jesus Today.* Edinburgh: T. & T. Clark, 1997.

Stott, John R. W. *Between Two Worlds: The Art of Preaching in the Twentieth Century.* Grand Rapids: Eerdmans, 1982.

Thoma, Clemens, and Michael Wyschogrod, eds. *Parable and Story in Judaism and Christianity.* Studies in Judaism and Christianity. New York: Paulist, 1989.

Tomlinson, Dave. *The Post-Evangelical.* London: Triangle (SPCK), 1995.

Tracy, David. *On Naming the Present: God, Hermeneutics, Church.* Concilium. Maryknoll, N.Y.: Orbis; London: SCM, 1994.

Veith, Gene Edward, Jr. *Postmodern Times: A Christian Guide to Contemporary Thought and Culture.* Turning Point Christian Worldview series. Wheaton, Ill.: Crossway, 1994.

Wallace, Ronald S. *The Gospel Miracles: Many Things in Parables.* Grand Rapids: Eerdmans, 1963.

Westermann, Claus. *The Parables of Jesus in the Light of the Old Testament.* Minneapolis: Fortress Press, 1990.

Westphal, Merold, ed. *Postmodernism—Religions Aspects.* Bloomington: Indiana University Press, 1999.

Wilder, Amos N. *Jesus' Parables and the War of Myths: Essays on Imagination in the Scripture.* London: SPCK, 1982.

Willson, A. Leslie, ed. *German Romantic Criticism: Novalis, Schlegel, Schleiermacher, and Others.* The German Library, vol. 21. New York: Continuum, 1982.

Young, Brad H. *The Parables: Jewish Tradition and Christian Interpretation.* Peabody, Mass.: Hendrickson, 1998.

Index of Biblical References